Letts

EDUCATIONAL

ADVANCED SUBSIDIARY

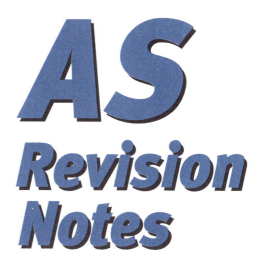

AS
Revision Notes

History

Modern British and European

Author

Michael Scaife

Contents

The age of reform, 1815–46

Lord Liverpool and the Tories, 1815–30

The causes of distress and discontent after 1815

- The main cause was **unemployment** because of the end of wartime contracts, the demobilisation of soldiers, the post-war slump, the effects of the industrial revolution and the displacement of rural workers by enclosure.
- Living and working conditions in the new **industrial towns** were poor.
- The **Corn Laws** (1815) kept the price of bread high.
- **Indirect taxes** were raised when income tax was abolished in 1816.

The government's response to discontent

- The government feared revolution, so it followed a policy of **repression**: suspension of Habeas Corpus, the Seditious Meetings Act (1817), the use of spies (e.g. Oliver) and of troops. This culminated in the **Six Acts** (1819).
- It opposed parliamentary reform and failed to introduce social reforms.

Assessment of government policies

- The government may have exaggerated the danger of revolution. Discontent was at its highest when economic conditions were worst.
- Some of its policies, e.g. the Corn Laws, the tax changes, the Game Laws and the use of spies, made matters worse.
- But the government was undoubtedly faced by disorder and it had no effective police force.

The Liberal Tories, 1822–30

The Liberal Tories introduced important reforms.

- **Peel** reformed the penal code, improved conditions in the bigger gaols and established the Metropolitan Police (1829).
- **Huskisson** introduced free trade measures: reduction of import duties, relaxation of the Navigation Acts and reciprocity agreements. He also modified the Corn Laws in 1828 by the introduction of a sliding scale.
- The Combination Acts were repealed (1824), with an Amending Act (1825).
- The Test and Corporation Acts were repealed (1828).
- **Catholic emancipation** was passed in 1829, but only because of the threat of civil war in Ireland. Moreover, it split the Tory Party.

Examiner's Tip

The liberalism of the Liberal Tories was limited: they would not consider parliamentary reform and upheld the Corn Laws.

The Great Reform Act, 1832

Parliamentary reform: faults of the unreformed parliament

- Qualifications for voting were outdated, arbitrary and illogical.
- The electorate was tiny – less than half a million.
- The South of England was **over-represented** and the North and Scotland were **under-represented**.
- There were many **rotten** and **pocket boroughs**.
- Growing industrial towns such as **Manchester** were unrepresented.
- There was no secret ballot, leading to bribery and intimidation of voters.

The opposition to reform

- Some opposition came from people who would lose out by reform, e.g. members of the House of Lords who were able to nominate MPs for pocket boroughs.
- Some argued that the present system worked perfectly well. All the important 'interests' in the country, e.g. landowners, merchants, the professions, were represented.
- Peel claimed that there would inevitably be demands for further reform.

The struggle for the Reform Act

- The split in the Tory Party over catholic emancipation led to the fall of Wellington in 1830 and a Whig government under **Grey**, who favoured limited reform.
- Fear of **revolution**, strengthened by the 1830 revolution in France and widespread disturbances in England in 1831–2, helped the Whigs to overcome the opposition.
- Three Bills had to be introduced and a general election held. The House of Lords finally passed the third Bill when Grey obtained a promise from the King to create enough peers to force it through if necessary.

The terms of the Reform Act

- The vote was given to **£10 householders** in the boroughs; in the counties the 40 shillings freeholders retained the right to vote, and it was also given to £50 leaseholders and £10 copyholders.
- Over 140 seats were redistributed from rotten and pocket boroughs to **growing towns and the larger counties**.

Results of the Act

- The electorate was still only about 800 000.
- The working classes were not enfranchised.
- Constituencies still varied greatly in size.
- The South of England was still over-represented.
- MPs were still largely drawn from the landowning class.
- But the Act did give many of the middle classes a vote, and governments and political parties had to take more account of their views.

Examiner's Tip

The importance of the Reform Act was that it set a precedent for changing the constitution and opened the way for future reforms of parliament.

The Whig reforms

- The abolition of slavery in the British Empire, 1833.
- The Factory Act (1833) restricted child labour in textile factories. Four **inspectors** were appointed. This was the first effective Factory Act.
- The first government grant for **education** (1833) – £20 000 to the National Society, and the British and Foreign Society.
- The Poor Law Amendment Act of 1834 (see below).
- The Municipal Corporations Act (1835) reformed local government in towns.
- Registration of births, marriages and deaths (1836).
- Church reforms: the Marriage Act and the Tithe Commutation Act (1836).
- The Whig reforms were a major step in adjusting central and local government to the needs of an industrialising society.

The Poor Law Amendment Act, 1834

- Under the old Poor Law each parish was responsible for its own poor. Poor relief was paid for by a parish rate levied by Overseers of the Poor.
- In southern England, under the **Speenhamland System**, the wages of agricultural labourers were supplemented by the Poor Law. This depressed wages and made labourers unable to escape dependence on the Poor Law.
- The cost of the Poor Law escalated.
- By the **Poor Law Amendment Act** outdoor relief was abolished, except for the sick and aged. This meant the end of the Speenhamland system.
- For the able-bodied poor, relief was to be provided in workhouses.
- The workhouses were to be run on the principle of **'less eligibility'**.
- Parishes were grouped into **Poor Law Unions** run by elected Boards of Guardians.
- A central Board of Commissioners was appointed to supervise the whole system. **Chadwick** was its secretary.

Results of the Act

- The new Poor Law reduced costs and was therefore popular with ratepayers.
- Conditions in the workhouses were harsh. The new Poor Law was therefore very unpopular with the working classes.
- In the industrial north it proved impossible to implement the new system in full. An **Anti-Poor Law movement** arose.
- In 1847 the Commissioners were replaced by the Poor Law Board, and after this there was a slow improvement in the treatment of children, the sick and the old.

Examiner's Tip

The Whig reforms were a response to the needs of an industrialising society but they were bitterly disappointing to the working classes, many of whom turned to Chartism.

The Chartist movement and the Anti-Corn Law League

The Chartist movement

- The aim of Chartism was a democratic parliament, to be achieved by the **Six Points** of the Charter. It sought political reform as a step towards a better society.
- The years of greatest Chartist activity were **1839, 1842 and 1848**, in each of which a petition was presented to parliament. All three petitions were rejected, and after 1848 support dwindled.
- Chartism was a movement of the industrial working class, protesting against their living and working conditions in the economic depression of the late 1830s and 1840s.
- It reflected working-class disappointment with the 1832 Reform Act and anger at the Poor Law Amendment Act and the collapse of Owen's Grand National Consolidated Trade Union.

Reasons for the failure of Chartism

- Poor leadership – Lovett, Attwood and O'Connor all had their differing faults.
- Divisions over tactics – Moral Force v. Physical Force.
- Lack of co-ordination, reflecting the local nature of much Chartist activity.
- Improving economic conditions from the mid-1840s (except in 1848).
- Firm action by the government.
- Lack of middle-class support.

The Anti-Corn Law League

- The League was formed in Manchester in 1839. Its sole aim was the repeal of the Corn Laws, which were the last main obstacle to **free trade**.
- It had middle-class leadership (**Cobden** and **Bright**, both of whom became MPs), and gained support from both the middle and working classes.
- It ran a highly-organised campaign, making good use of the press.
- It argued that free trade would reduce the price of bread, enable British manufacturers to expand exports and thus increase employment, make agriculture more efficient by exposing it to foreign competition, and promote international peace through trade.
- The landed interest, which dominated the Conservative Party, claimed that repeal would lead to an influx of cheap foreign corn, ruining farmers and causing unemployment in the countryside.
- The campaign against the Corn Laws, therefore, had a **political** as well as an economic significance: it was a struggle by the industrial middle classes against the continuing influence of the landed aristocracy.

Examiner's Tip

The Chartist movement was an important step towards the organisation of an effective working-class movement. The Anti-Corn Law League, with strong middle-class support, had more immediate success.

Peel

- Peel was Chief Secretary for Ireland from 1812–18, Chairman of the **Bullion Committee** in 1819, and Home Secretary 1822–27 and 1828–30.
- In 1829 he played a crucial role in bringing about **Catholic emancipation**. Many Tories attacked him for betraying the Church.
- He opposed the 1832 Reform Act, but in December 1834 he issued the **Tamworth Manifesto,** which said that the Tory Party accepted that the Reform Act could not be reversed and would seek to reform proved abuses.
- He was **Prime Minister** in 1834–35, but lost the 1835 election despite the Tamworth Manifesto.
- He won a convincing victory in the election of 1841. By then he had won the confidence of the new electorate.

Peel's second ministry, 1841–46: reforms

- The budgets of 1842 and 1845 were a major step towards **free trade** and helped to bring about a trade revival.
- He reintroduced income tax – for three years at first, but it was then renewed.
- The Bank Charter Act (1844) stabilised the banking system and the currency.
- The Companies Act (1844) established better regulation of companies.
- There were two social reforms – the Mines Act (1842) and the Factory Act (1844).

Ireland

- Faced by the challenge from **'Young Ireland'**, O'Connell held a series of meetings to demand repeal of the Act of Union, culminating in a mass meeting at Clontarf in 1843. Peel banned the meeting.
- He appointed the **Devon Commission** to investigate the Irish land problem, but was unable to act on its report before the fall of his ministry.
- He increased the government grant to **Maynooth College**. In 1845 a more serious problem arose in Ireland: the potato famine.

The repeal of the Corn Laws, 1846

- Peel played the decisive role in bringing about repeal. He was already committed to free trade but knew that repeal of the Corn Laws would split the Conservative Party.
- The **Irish famine** made him decide to act. The Repeal Bill was passed with the support of the Whigs and a minority of Conservatives.
- Peel was accused by Disraeli of betraying his party. Shortly afterwards his ministry was defeated and he was forced to resign.
- The Repeal of the Corn Laws was **a turning point in British politics**. It was disastrous for the Conservatives. The Peelites, led by Gladstone, eventually joined the Whigs to form the Liberal Party.
- British agriculture, contrary to the landowners' fears, entered a period of prosperity – until the depression of the 1870s.

Examiner's Tip

Consider two views of Peel: (a) he was a great statesman who put the national interest before his party; (b) he was a poor party leader who betrayed the party over corn, cash and Catholics.

Progress check

1 What measures introduced by the government in 1815–16 added to the discontent of the working classes?

2 What was the effect of the suspension of Habeas Corpus in 1817?

3 What measures did Huskisson introduce to assist trade?

4 Why did Peel and Wellington introduce Catholic emancipation in 1829?

5 What were the main faults in the distribution of seats in parliament before 1832?

6 What were the qualifications for voting after 1832?

7 What did Peel claim would be the result of reforming parliament?

8 How far did the 1832 Reform Act lead to a change in the type of people who became MPs?

9 Why was the Factory Act of 1833 more important than previous Factory Acts?

10 How big was the first government grant for education and to whom was it given?

11 What was the Speenhamland system?

12 What was meant by the principle of 'less eligibility'?

13 Who were the leaders of the Anti-Corn Law League?

14 How did the Anti-Corn Law League think repeal of the Corn Laws would affect international relations?

15 Who were the main leaders of the Chartist movement?

16 What is meant by calling Chartism a 'knife and fork question'?

17 What pledges did Peel make in the Tamworth Manifesto?

18 What were the most important measures introduced by Peel in his budgets?

19 Why did some Conservatives oppose the increased grant to Maynooth College?

20 Why was the repeal of the Corn Laws opposed by the majority of the Conservative Party?

Answers on page 88

England, 1846–86

Politics, 1846–68

The political parties

- The split in the Conservative Party over the repeal of the Corn Laws produced a confused political situation.
- The **Whigs** dominated politics. They held office under either Russell or Palmerston as Prime Minister during the years 1846–52, 1855–58 and 1859–66.
- The decision of Gladstone to accept office as Chancellor of the Exchequer under Palmerston in 1859 was the turning point in the evolution of the Whig Party into the **Liberal Party**, consisting of Whigs, Peelites and Radicals.
- There were three short **Conservative minority governments** in 1852, 1858–59 and 1866–68, but they did not win a general election until 1874.

Personalities

- **Palmerston** was either Foreign Secretary or Prime Minister for most of the period 1846–1865. His willingness to stand up for British interests made him popular and helps to explain the political dominance of the Whigs.
- Foreign affairs was his main concern. He had little interest in domestic affairs and saw little need for reform. He opposed parliamentary reform.
- **Gladstone** supported Peel over the repeal of the Corn Laws. As Chancellor of the Exchequer in 1852–1855 and 1859–66, he completed the move to free trade.
- **Disraeli** led the attack on Peel over the repeal of the Corn Laws. He was the outstanding figure in the Conservative Party over the next twenty years but he was mistrusted.
- In the three Derby ministries of 1852, 1858–59 and 1866–68 Disraeli served as Chancellor of the Exchequer.

The Second Reform Act, 1867

- The vote was extended to male householders and £10 lodgers in the boroughs and to £12 leaseholders in the counties.
- 45 seats were redistributed to large counties and growing towns.
- The electorate almost doubled from 1.36 to 2.5 million. Since most of the new voters were from the **urban working class**, it was an important step towards democracy, though still short of full democracy.
- The Act also marked an important stage in the development of political parties because in the larger boroughs the electorate was too big to bribe. It was therefore necessary to have an efficient **local organisation**.
- It was Disraeli's greatest parliamentary triumph but the immediate benefit went to Gladstone, who won the 1868 election.

Examiner's Tip

The split in the Conservative Party in 1846 led to a realignment of the political parties by 1868.

Gladstone

Gladstonian Liberalism

The basic principles of Gladstonian Liberalism were:

- Free trade.
- *Laissez faire* – the government should not intervene in the economy.
- Strict economy in government finance.
- Equality of opportunity and hostility to privilege.
- A peaceful foreign policy based on respect for other countries.

Gladstone's first ministry, 1868–74:

Domestic reforms

- Forster's Education Act (1870) provided for elementary schools (Board Schools) to be set up and funded from the rates. Religious education was to be non-denominational. Existing Church Schools would receive increased government grants.
- The University Tests Act (1871) opened teaching posts at Oxford and Cambridge to non-conformists.
- The civil service reforms (1871) provided that posts were to be filled by competitive examination rather than by recommendation by an MP or a peer.
- The Trade Union Act (1871) gave unions legal recognition, but the Criminal Law Amendment Act made picketing – even peaceful picketing – illegal.
- The Ballot Act (1872) instituted secret ballots in elections, thus reducing bribery and intimidation.
- Cardwell's army reforms reorganised the regiments and the administration of the army and abolished flogging and the purchase of commissions.
- The Licensing Act (1872) gave magistrates the power to reduce the number of pubs.
- The Judicature Act (1872) reorganised the law courts.

Foreign policy

- Gladstone could only protest ineffectively at a conference held in London (1871) when Russia renounced the Black Sea clauses of the Treaty of Paris of 1856.
- In 1872 he agreed to pay compensation to the USA for the damage caused to shipping in the American Civil War by the *Alabama*.

Gladstone's second ministry, 1880–85: domestic policies

- There was comparatively little reform in Gladstone's second ministry partly because of Gladstone's involvement with the Irish problem and partly because the Liberal Party was divided about the need for social reform.
- The Reform and Redistribution Acts (1884–85) gave the vote to all male householders in the counties and redistributed 147 seats from smaller boroughs to more populous areas. This was an important step towards full democracy, but women and about 40 per cent of men were still without the vote.

Examiner's Tip

Gladstone's first ministry reduced privilege and made Britain a more efficiently run country but it failed to tackle social reform. Many of its reforms aroused opposition.

Gladstone and Ireland, 1868–85

Irish grievances

- The established **church** was the Protestant Church of Ireland. The majority of the Irish were Roman Catholics.
- Much of the **land** was divided into small plots rented from English absentee landlords. Irish tenants had no security of tenure and no incentive to improve their holdings.
- The **Act of Union** (1800) had abolished Ireland's parliament. A demand arose for Home Rule. In 1870, Isaac Butt founded the **Home Rule League**.

Gladstone's first ministry

- When Gladstone came to power in 1868, he was determined to try to 'pacify Ireland'.
- In 1869 the **Irish Church Act** disestablished the Church of Ireland.
- By the **First Irish Land Act** (1870), evicted tenants were to be compensated for improvements, unless evicted for non-payment of rent. But there was nothing to stop landlords raising rents to unaffordable levels.

The Home Rule League and the Irish Land League

- After 1873, when the agricultural depression began, evictions increased.
- In 1877 **Parnell** took over leadership of the Home Rule League.
- In 1879 **Michael Davitt** founded the Irish Land League, which organised a campaign of rent strikes and boycotts.
- The Home Rule League, the Land League and the Fenians came together in **the New Departure** – using militant tactics to pressurise the government.

Gladstone's second ministry

- The **Second Land Act** (1881) granted Irish tenants the three Fs: fair rents, fixity of tenure and free sale of the lease.
- At the same time, a Coercion Act was passed to control the violence.
- To keep up the pressure on Gladstone, Parnell through the Land League organised a campaign of non-payment of rent. Gladstone then ordered his arrest.
- After six months he made an agreement with him, the **Kilmainham 'Treaty' (1882)**. Parnell called off the rent strike and Gladstone promised an Arrears Bill.
- Four days later the **Phoenix Park murders** took place. This act of terrorism convinced many people in England that the Irish were not fit to govern themselves.
- It convinced Gladstone that only Home Rule would pacify Ireland. But he realised that he would need to move cautiously to win support and to avoid a split in the Liberal Party.

Examiner's Tip

By 1885 Gladstone had failed to 'pacify Ireland'. The Irish view was that his measures were 'too little, too late'.

Gladstone and Ireland: Home Rule

The First Home Rule Bill, 1886

- The 1885 general election gave Parnell's Irish Home Rule party the balance of power in the House of Commons.
- Gladstone's son then revealed his father's conversion to Home Rule.
- Parnell therefore gave the support of the Irish MPs to Gladstone, who formed his third ministry in 1886.
- The **First Home Rule Bill** proposed a parliament in Dublin to deal with Irish domestic affairs, and that there would be no Irish MPs at Westminster.
- The Home Rule Bill split the Liberal party: 93 Liberals, led by **Joseph Chamberlain** and Hartington, voted against the bill which was defeated in the Commons.
- The split in the Liberal party ushered in twenty years of largely Conservative government, during which the Liberal Unionists (those Liberals who had voted against Home Rule) moved over to become allies of the Conservatives.

The Second Home Rule Bill, 1893

- In 1892 Gladstone, with Irish support, formed his fourth ministry. The **Second Home Rule Bill** (1893) differed from the first in that it proposed that there should be Irish MPs at Westminster.
- The Bill passed the Commons but was heavily defeated in the Lords, where there was a Conservative majority. Gladstone then retired in 1894.

The fall of Parnell

- Parnell was accused in letters published in *The Times* of being involved in the Phoenix Park murders. A commission of enquiry in 1890 concluded that they had been forged by Pigott. Parnell was at the height of his power.
- But then his authority was undermined by the **O'Shea divorce**. His downfall and his death a year later left the Irish nationalists divided and weak.

Why did Gladstone fail to achieve Home Rule for Ireland?

- The Liberal Party split over the issue.
- The **House of Lords**, dominated by landowners, many with land in Ireland, was overwhelmingly opposed.
- There was opposition from **Protestants in Ulster**, who claimed that Home Rule would mean 'Rome rule'.
- Many people, e.g. Chamberlain, believed that Home Rule would stir up demands for independence in other territories in the British Empire.
- The Irish Nationalists were weakened by the downfall of Parnell.

Examiner's Tip

Despite the failure of the Home Rule Bills, Ireland in 1894 was relatively quiet, partly because of the downfall of Parnell and partly because a scheme to help tenants purchase their land had been introduced.

Disraeli

'Tory Democracy'

- Disraeli's political ideas, sometimes called 'Tory democracy', were intended to appeal to the new electorate created by the 1867 Reform Act.
- Disraeli stressed the central role of the monarchy, the aristocracy and the Church in national life.
- He promised that a Conservative government would pursue a policy of social reform on the paternalist ground that the rich should help the poor.
- The Conservatives would also develop the Empire (imperialism).

Disraeli's second ministry, 1874–80

Domestic affairs

- The **Public Health Act** (1875) imposed a range of duties on local authorities, e.g. supply of clean water, removal of sewage and nuisances.
- The Artisans' Dwellings Act (1875) gave the local authorities power to clear **slums**, though they were not compelled to do so.
- The Factory Act (1874) reduced the working day to **ten hours** and raised the minimum age for the employment of children to ten.
- The Conspiracy and Protection of Property Act (1875) made **peaceful picketing** legal.
- The Employers and Workmen Act (1876) made breach of contract by a worker a civil offence, as it was for an employer.
- The Education Act (1876) set up School Attendance Committees to encourage attendance, though it was still not compulsory.
- Other reforms were the Sale of Food and Drugs Act, the Rivers Pollution Act and the Merchant Shipping Act.

Foreign and imperial affairs

- In the **Balkan crisis of 1875–78**, Disraeli wished to follow the traditional British policy of supporting Turkey as a bulwark against Russian expansion. Turkish brutality, which provoked a savage denunciation by Gladstone, made this difficult. But when Russia intervened and threatened Constantinople, Disraeli sent the British fleet and threatened war.
- In the end he was able, in co-operation with Bismarck, to put pressure on Russia to agree to the **Congress of Berlin (1878)**. This was a triumph for Disraeli. The settlement which Russia had imposed on Turkey was considerably modified and Britain gained **Cyprus**.
- In imperial affairs, he purchased the **Suez Canal shares** in 1875, and in 1876 he created the title **Empress of India** for Queen Victoria.

In 1878–79, Disraeli's 'forward' policies led to the outbreak of the **Afghan and Zulu Wars**, in both of which British troops suffered defeats before they were eventually successful. Public opinion began to see Disraeli's imperialism as dangerous, and this contributed to his defeat in 1880.

Examiner's Tip

Disraeli's second ministry produced a substantial record of social reform, much of which was the work of the Home Secretary, Cross. The weakness was that many of the Acts were permissive.

Progress check

ENGLAND, 1846–86

1. How did the repeal of the Corn Laws affect the Conservative Party?
2. What was the political importance of Gladstone's appointment as Chancellor of the Exchequer in 1859?
3. Why was Palmerston popular with the general public?
4. How did the Second Reform Act affect party organisation?
5. Why did nonconformists object to the Education Act of 1870?
6. What effect did the Criminal Law Amendment Act have on the activities of trade unions? And how did it affect Gladstone's popularity with their members?
7. How did Gladstone's reforms reduce privilege?
8. Which classes of people were given the vote by (a) the 1867 Reform Act; (b) the 1884 Reform Act?
9. How did Gladstone attempt to settle Irish land grievances by (a) the First Land Act of 1870; (b) the Second Land Act of 1881?
10. What tactics were employed by the Irish Land League and the Home Rule Association in the late 1870s and early 1880s?
11. What undertakings did Gladstone and Parnell give in the Kilmainham Treaty?
12. What was the impact of the Phoenix Park murders on English public opinion?
13. How did the First Home Rule Bill affect the Liberal Party?
14. Why did Parnell lose his hold on Irish nationalism in 1890?
15. In which House of Parliament was (a) the First Home Rule Bill and (b) the Second Home Rule Bill defeated?
16. Why was there opposition to Home Rule in Ulster?
17. In what ways did the attitudes of Gladstone and Disraeli towards social reform differ?
18. What was the effect of the Conspiracy and Protection of Property Act?
19. Why may the Congress of Berlin be regarded as a triumph for Disraeli?
20. How did Disraeli's imperialism contribute to his defeat in the 1880 election?

Answers on page 88

AS History Revision Notes

15

Foreign affairs, 1815–1902

Castlereagh and Canning

Castlereagh's aims

- Promoting British **trade**, which in turn depended on a powerful navy.
- Maintaining **the balance of power** in Europe, which would preserve peace and thus help to promote trade.
- Keeping a close watch on Russia and France, which Castlereagh saw as the main threats to the balance of power.

The Vienna Settlement, 1815

- Castlereagh tried to ensure that France was treated firmly but not vindictively and that the balance of power in Europe was maintained.
- Buffer states were built up around France to guard against future aggression.
- Britain gained colonies which were valuable for trade or as naval bases.

The Congress System

- Castlereagh and Metternich, the Austrian Chancellor, wanted to set up a permanent system of consultation between the great powers – a **Concert of Europe**.
- In the **Quadruple Alliance** of 1815, Britain, Austria, Prussia and Russia agreed to hold regular congresses to discuss threats to peace.
- Castlereagh disapproved of Tsar Alexander I's Holy Alliance.
- At the Congress of **Aix-la-Chapelle** (1818): France was admitted to the Quintuple Alliance and the army of occupation was withdrawn.
- At **Troppau** (1820) the continental powers asserted their right to intervene in revolutions (the Troppau Protocol). Castlereagh in his **State Paper of 1820** opposed intervention in the internal affairs of other countries.
- He only sent an observer to **Laibach** (1821). By 1822 Britain was on the verge of dropping out of the Congress System.

Canning

- Canning withdrew from the **Congress of Verona** (1822).
- He prevented Spanish intervention in **Portugal** by sending a naval squadron to help the Liberals to win control.
- In 1825 he recognised the independence of **Mexico, Colombia and Argentina**. His main motive was to promote British trading interests.
- In the **Greek Revolt (1821–1830)**, Canning acted jointly with Russia and France with the aim of forcing Turkey to grant self-rule to Greece.
- After Canning's death, Wellington failed to continue this policy. Greece gained full independence and Russia's influence in the Balkans was increased, which was what Canning had tried to prevent.

Examiner's Tip

Canning shared Castlereagh's aims but his style was different. He appeared more favourable to liberal movements and he was better at winning public support.

Palmerston

Palmerston's foreign policy, 1830–41

- Palmerston aimed to protect British trading interests, to maintain peace and the balance of power, and to uphold British prestige. He supported liberal and national movements provided they did not conflict with British interests. He was suspicious of Russia and France.

- In **Belgium** his aim was to prevent France gaining too much influence. Working with Louis Philippe, he ensured that Belgium became independent and neutral. In 1839 the Treaty of London guaranteed Belgian neutrality.

- In **Spain and Portugal**, he succeeded in preserving constitutional governments while preventing France from gaining too much influence.

- In **the Near East** he feared the growth of Russian power at the expense of Turkey. The Treaty of Unkiar Skelessi (1833) particularly worried him. He was eventually successful in resolving the problem by the **Straits Convention** (1841), by which the Dardanelles was closed to warships of all nations in peacetime.

- He took advantage of a dispute over the import of opium into China to provoke the **Opium War** and force the Chinese to open five ports to British trade.

Palmerston's foreign policy, 1846–51

- In the affair of the **Spanish marriages** (1846) he was outwitted by Louis Philippe.

- In 1848 he sympathised with the revolutionaries, especially in Italy, but he also regarded a strong Austria as important to act as a counter-balance to Russia.

- His handling of the visit of Haynau to London and the **Don Pacifico affair** both won popular approval but brought him into conflict with the Queen.

- His approval of Louis Napoleon's coup d'état in 1851 so angered her that she demanded that Russell should dismiss him.

Foreign affairs under Palmerston as Prime Minister, 1855–65

- He brought the **Crimean War** to a successful end for Britain. By the Treaty of Paris (1856) the Black Sea was neutralised.

- In the Chinese Wars (1856–60), he forced China to open several more ports to trade.

- He played a part in the **unification of Italy** in 1859–60. He used his influence in favour of the union of Parma, Modena and Tuscany with Piedmont. In 1860, his refusal to intervene allowed Garibaldi to cross from Sicily to the Italian mainland.

- His handling of the problems created by the American Civil War was clumsy. He nearly provoked a war with the North by his handling of the *'Trent'* incident. There was further friction when he refused to pay compensation for the damage to Northern shipping inflicted by the *'Alabama'*.

- In the Polish Revolt of 1863, he unwisely led the Poles to expect British help, but had to back down in the face of Russia's determination.

- Over **Schleswig-Holstein (1864)**, he threatened war in support of Denmark but was outmanoeuvred by Bismarck, who realised that he was bluffing.

Examiner's Tip

Palmerston pursued British prestige and asserted Britain's influence in Europe with great success. By the 1860s, however, he was increasingly out of his depth in a changing Europe.

The Eastern Question

- The Eastern Question arose from the decline of the Turkish (or Ottoman) Empire, which in 1815 still ruled much of south-east Europe.
- Britain was particularly suspicious of Russia, which not only had racial (Slav) and religious (Orthodox) sympathies with the peoples of the Balkans, but also wanted access to the Mediterranean from the Black Sea for its fleet. This would endanger Britain's trading interests in the eastern Mediterranean and its route to India.

The Crimean War, 1854–56

- The immediate cause of the war was a dispute between France and Russia over the guardianship of the **Holy Places**, which gave rise to a Russian claim to protect all Christians in the Ottoman Empire. When this demand was rejected, the Russians invaded Moldavia and Wallachia and a war between Russia and Turkey ensued.
- When part of the Turkish fleet was sunk at **Sinope**, public opinion in Britain and France demanded war.
- The Russians evacuated Moldavia and Wallachia and the British and French then sent forces to the Crimea. After victories at the battles of the Alma, Balaclava and Inkerman, they captured the Russian naval base at Sebastopol.
- By the Treaty of Paris (1856), **the Black Sea was neutralised**, which meant that Russia was not allowed to have a navy there. Moldavia, Wallachia and Serbia gained a large degree of independence.

The Balkan Crisis, 1875–78

- There were revolts against Turkish rule in Bosnia, Herzegovina and Bulgaria in 1875–76.
- Disraeli feared Russian intervention, but Turkish brutality in suppressing the revolts, which was denounced by Gladstone, made it difficult to support Turkey.
- Tsar Alexander II declared war on Turkey (1877). When Russian troops approached Constantinople, the traditional British fear of Russian expansion into the Mediterranean was aroused. Disraeli sent a fleet to Constantinople.
- Russia then made peace with Turkey (the **Treaty of San Stefano 1878**); this set up a 'big' Bulgaria, which Disraeli feared would be under Russian control.
- Working with Bismarck, he put pressure on Russia to agree to the **Congress of Berlin (1878)**, as a result of which Bulgaria was reduced in size. Eastern Roumelia was given autonomy within the Turkish Empire and Macedonia was returned to Turkey. Britain gained Cyprus.

The Mediterranean Agreements, 1887

- In 1885 Eastern Roumelia declared itself united with Bulgaria. Salisbury accepted this since Bulgaria had proved to be more independent than expected.
- In 1887 he negotiated the Mediterranean Agreements with Italy and Austria by which the three powers agreed to maintain the status quo in the Mediterranean.

Examiner's Tip

The Congress of Berlin was a triumph for Disraeli. He checked Russian ambitions without a war and bolstered Turkey.

Imperialism

- The 'New Imperialism' of the late nineteenth century claimed that expansion of the empire would help the economy by providing markets for exports, outlets for investment and sources of raw materials for industry.
- It would also help to reduce over-population by emigration, bring the benefits of civilisation to backward peoples and spread Christianity.
- The 'scramble for Africa' made imperialism competitive: national prestige demanded that each major imperial power should not allow its rivals to gain more than it did itself.
- The scramble for Africa was a means by which European powers worked out their rivalries without going to war in Europe.

Disraeli and the Empire

- In 1875 Disraeli purchased the Suez Canal shares and in 1876 he created the title 'Empress of India' for Queen Victoria.
- In 1878–79 his 'forward' policies led to the Afghan and Zulu Wars. In both of these, British troops suffered defeats before they were eventually successful.

Chamberlain and the Empire

- Chamberlain took the post of **Colonial Secretary** in 1895 because he regarded it as so important.
- He encouraged investment in the colonies, e.g. in railways.
- He wanted to develop the Empire into a single economic and political unit.

Egypt and the Sudan

- Disraeli's purchase of shares in the Suez Canal in 1875 began Britain's involvement in **Egypt**. Growing disorder in Egypt led Gladstone to order its occupation in 1881. Egypt came under British control, although it was not annexed.
- Gladstone decided to abandon the Sudan but this led to the death of **General Gordon** at Khartoum, for which Gladstone was blamed by public opinion.
- In 1896 Chamberlain sent an expedition under Kitchener to reconquer the Sudan. This led to a confrontation with the French at **Fashoda**. In the end, the French withdrew. In 1904, they recognised Egypt and the Sudan as a British sphere of influence.

The Berlin Conference of 1884–85

- France, Germany and Italy acquired colonies in Africa in the 1880s. Inevitably disputes arose.
- The **Berlin Conference** of 1884–85 agreed that any power which effectively occupied African territory would become its possessor. This gave the green light for Africa to be carved up.
- Between 1884 and 1896 Britain acquired Somaliland, Nigeria, the interior of the Gold Coast, Kenya, Uganda, Bechuanaland, Nyasaland and Rhodesia.
- In 1890 Salisbury negotiated a series of colonial agreements with France, Germany and Portugal.

Examiner's Tip

Britain acquired extensive colonial territories in the 'scramble for Africa', but colonial disputes with other powers were settled without war.

The Second Boer War 1899–1902

Britain and the Boers

- The Boer republics of Transvaal and the Orange Free State had their origin in the desire of the Boers to escape from British rule (the **Great Trek**, 1835–37).
- In 1877 the Boers of the Transvaal accepted a British protectorate because of the threat from the Zulus.
- In the **Zulu War** of 1879 the British were at first defeated at Isandhlwana but were eventually victorious. The Boers then demanded the restoration of their independence. After a short war (the **First Boer War, 1881**) Gladstone, who was not an imperialist, agreed to this.

Causes of the Second Boer War

- In 1886 gold was discovered in the Transvaal. Thousand of foreigners, mainly British, flocked to the Transvaal.
- By 1895 these **'uitlanders'** outnumbered the Boers, but they had no political rights and were heavily taxed. They had genuine grievances which the Boers, who resented their presence, did little to meet.
- The scramble for Africa left the Boer republics almost encircled. In 1884, Cecil Rhodes set up a British protectorate over Bechuanaland and in 1889 he formed the British South Africa Company to develop colonies in Rhodesia (modern Zimbabwe and Zambia). Rhodes envisaged British colonies from southern Africa to Egypt (the **Cape to Cairo Railway**). His activities aroused deep suspicion among the Boers. In 1890 he became Prime Minister of Cape Colony.
- The **Jameson Raid** (1895), for which Rhodes was responsible (and in which Chamberlain was implicated), heightened tension.
- Talks on the Uitlander question in 1899, between **Milner**, the British High Commissioner, who completely mistrusted the Boers, and **Kruger** the President of Transvaal, broke down. War broke out when the Boers attacked Natal.

The War

- After initial setbacks, the British gained military superiority by 1900 but it took two more years to wear down resistance by Boer guerilla groups. One of the methods used by the British in this phase of the war was the establishment of concentration camps.
- By the **Treaty of Vereeniging** (1902), Transvaal and the Orange Free State were annexed but were promised eventual self-government which was granted in 1906.
- In 1910 they were joined with Cape Colony and Natal in the **Union of South Africa**.

Examiner's Tip

The war exposed Britain's diplomatic isolation. All the other great powers sympathised with the Boers.

Progress check

1 Which four powers were the original members of the Congress System?

2 Explain (a) the Troppau Protocol and (b) the British State Paper of 1820.

3 What was the main business of the Congress of Aix-la-Chapelle?

4 Identify two ways in which Canning differed from Castlereagh in his conduct of foreign affairs.

5 Why did Canning think it was in Britain's interests to recognise the independence of Spain's former colonies in South America?

6 Which two great powers did Palmerston regard with most suspicion?

7 What was the main provision of the Treaty of London (1839)?

8 Why did Palmerston think the Treaty of Unkiar Skelessi was contrary to British interests?

9 What did he achieve by the Straits Convention of 1841?

10 Why did Palmerston not provide active support for the 1848 revolutions despite his sympathy for liberal and national movements?

11 What did the Treaty of Paris (1856) say about the Black Sea?

12 What were the views of Gladstone and Disraeli about the Balkan Crisis of 1875–78?

13 Why did Disraeli object to the Treaty of San Stefano?

14 What economic benefits did 'New Imperialism' expect from the expansion of the Empire?

15 What was Chamberlain's vision for the Empire?

16 What was the main outcome of the Berlin Conference of 1884–85?

17 What happened at Fashoda?

18 What was the 'uitlander' problem?

19 What was the effect of the Jameson Raid on Anglo-Boer relations?

20 Why did the Boer republics feel threatened by the activities of Cecil Rhodes?

Answers on page 89

The Edwardian age

The Conservatives, 1895–1905

Salisbury's third ministry

- The formation of Salisbury's third ministry in 1895 marked an important political development: the Liberal Unionists joined the Conservatives.
- Apart from the Prime Minister, the outstanding figure was **Joseph Chamberlain**. His period as Colonial Secretary marked the high point of British imperialism.
- Chamberlain wanted to introduce old age pensions but failed to persuade Salisbury. The only social reform was the Workmen's Compensation Act of 1897.

The retreat from 'Splendid Isolation'

By 1900 isolation had come to seem dangerous rather than splendid.

- The Fashoda Incident nearly caused a war with France.
- Anglo-German relations began to deteriorate in 1896, when Kaiser William II congratulated Kruger, the President of Transvaal, on repelling the **Jameson Raid**
- The **Boer War** exposed Britain's diplomatic isolation. Pro-Boer attitudes in Germany during the war did nothing to improve relations.
- The **German Naval Laws** of 1898 and 1900 seemed to threaten Britain's naval supremacy, on which its security depended.
- In 1902 Britain allied with **Japan**, which provided a safeguard against Russian expansion in the Far East.
- Britain sought an agreement with Germany, but was rebuffed in 1898–99.
- In 1904 Britain signed the **Entente Cordiale** with France. France recognised British control in Egypt, while Britain accepted France's ambitions in Morocco.

Balfour's ministry, 1902–05

- Balfour's ministry produced one major reform: the **Education Act of 1902**.
- Chamberlain resigned from the government in 1903 to conduct a campaign for **tariff reform**, which split the Conservative Party.

The 1906 election

The reasons for the overwhelming Liberal victory were:

- Tariff reform, which the Liberals attacked on the ground that it would lead to dearer food.
- There was a demand for social reform, which the Conservatives had failed to meet.
- The Taff Vale case alienated trade unionists.
- Nonconformists were angry about the 1902 Education Act.
- There was public indignation about the Chinese labour scandal.

Examiner's Tip

Chamberlain's tariff reform campaign was probably the crucial reason for the defeat of the Conservatives. He is the only politician to have split two major parties.

The Liberals, 1905–15

New Liberalism

- New Liberalism advocated social reform, financed by higher taxes on the wealthy. The social surveys of Booth and Rowntree had revealed the extent of poverty. The New Liberals believed state intervention was necessary to deal with this.

- New Liberalism advocated collectivist solutions to social problems, as opposed to Gladstonian Liberalism, which was individualist.

- The New Liberals saw social reform as the way to attract working-class votes and to avoid being outflanked by the recently formed Labour Party.

- By 1905 the New Liberals had probably won over the majority of the party. The outstanding New Liberal ministers were Lloyd George and Churchill.

The Liberal reforms

- **Trade unions:** The Trade Disputes Act (1906) reversed the Taff Vale judgement and freed unions from liability to pay damages for employers' losses in a strike. The Trade Union Act (1913) gave them the right to add a 'political levy' to their members' subscriptions, though members were allowed to 'contract out'.

- The **Children's Charter** comprised several measures to help the children of the poor: medical inspections in schools, free school meals for poor children and juvenile courts and special corrective schools (borstals) to keep child offenders out of adult law courts and prisons.

- **Working people**: In 1909, Churchill set up employment exchanges to help the unemployed find jobs. The Trade Boards Act set up boards to fix minimum wages in the 'sweated' industries, where there were no trade unions.

- The **Old Age Pensions Act** (1908) provided small pensions at 70 for the very poorest old people. The pensions were financed out of taxation.

- The **National Insurance Act** of 1911 provided insurance against sickness for all workers earning less than £160 per year, though not for their wives or families. It was a contributory scheme, financed by payments from workers, employers and the state. There was also an unemployment insurance scheme, financed in the same way, for workers in certain industries such as building, shipbuilding and engineering (the industries where demand for labour fluctuated most).

Assessment

- These measures relieved the worst effects of poverty and involved an increased role for the state. But they also fell short of a comprehensive system of social security.

- Some of the reforms were limited in scope. The old age pensions were very small and paid to only the very poorest. Unemployment insurance covered only a small proportion of the workforce.

- Nothing was done about the Poor Law. The Royal Commission on the Poor Law produced two reports. The Majority Report proposed reform of the Poor Law, the Minority Report proposed abolition. Neither was acted upon.

Examiner's Tip

The Liberals tried to make sure that the state provided minimum standards of social services and thus laid the foundation for the welfare state.

The House of Lords and Ireland

The 1909 Budget and the struggle with the Lords

- Apart from the law lords and the bishops, the House of Lords consisted entirely of hereditary peers, two-thirds of whom were Conservatives.
- The Lords rejected Gladstone's Second Home Rule Bill in 1893 but did not interfere with any Conservative bills between 1895 and 1905. After the Liberal victory in 1906, Balfour used the Conservative majority in the Lords to obstruct Liberal policies. The hereditary House was thus thwarting the will of the electorate.
- Matters came to a head with Lloyd George's 1909 budget. To pay for pensions and for building Dreadnoughts he proposed increased taxes on the wealthy, including a **tax on land values** which was particularly objectionable to landowners.
- The Lords rejected the budget. This was unprecedented and caused a **constitutional crisis**.

The Parliament Act, 1911

- After a general election in January 1910, the Lords accepted the budget.
- The Liberals were now determined to limit the powers of the Lords.
- After a prolonged struggle involving a second general election and a promise by the King to create up to 500 new peers, the Lords accepted the Parliament Act.
- Under the Act, the Lords lost the power to reject money bills, and their power to reject other bills was replaced by a **two-year delaying power**. The interval between general elections was reduced to five years.

Ireland

- The Parliament Act made it possible to force Home Rule through against the will of the Lords. The Irish Nationalists supported it in the expectation that Home Rule would be their reward.
- The elections of 1910 gave them the balance of power in the House of Commons.
- A Home Rule Bill was introduced in 1912 and became law in 1914 under the Parliament Act.

The Ulster Problem

- As a result, a militant Unionist movement arose in Ulster under the leadership of **Carson**. In 1912 he set up the Ulster Volunteers to prepare for armed resistance to Home Rule. The nationalists responded by forming the Irish Volunteers.
- The **'Curragh Mutiny'** in March 1914 showed that the government could not rely on the army to enforce Home Rule.
- Both sides smuggled arms into Ireland in 1914. Ireland seemed on the verge of civil war. Only the outbreak of the First World War prevented it.
- Asquith mishandled the Irish problem. He should have been firmer in banning private armies and arms imports. The Conservative leader, Bonar Law, was also to blame for encouraging Ulster Unionist preparations for armed resistance.

Examiner's Tip

The Parliament Act was a triumph for democracy. It ensured that in the end the will of the elected House of Parliament would prevail over the hereditary House.

Britain and the First World War

Britain and the outbreak of war in 1914

- In the **Algeciras Conference** on Morocco in 1906, Britain supported France. Germany's clumsy diplomacy strengthened the Anglo-French Entente.

- In 1907 an agreement was made with Russia to settle differences over Persia, Afghanistan and Tibet. This created the **Triple Entente.** But Britain was not committed to go to war as an ally of France and Russia.

- The **naval race** intensified as both Britain and Germany built Dreadnoughts.

- Haldane's mission to Berlin in 1912 to propose a cut in the naval building programme was unsuccessful and Churchill's suggestion in 1913 of a 'naval holiday' was also rejected.

- The **second Morocco crisis** (1911), when the German gunboat 'Panther' was sent to Agadir, provoked Britain to threaten war (Lloyd George's Mansion House speech). Germany backed down, though with some 'compensation' in the Congo.

- The crisis strengthened the Anglo-French Entente and led to the **Anglo-French Naval Agreement** (1912).

- In 1914 Britain was still not firmly committed to an alliance with France and Russia. The German invasion of Belgium tipped the balance.

The effects of the war on the political parties

- The war was a major factor in the decline of the Liberals. In 1915, **Asquith** formed a coalition. The energy of Lloyd George, as Minister of Munitions, contrasted markedly with Asquith's detachment.

- In December 1916, with Conservative support, **Lloyd George** forced Asquith to resign and became Prime Minister. The Liberal Party remained split between supporters of Lloyd George and of Asquith until 1923, by which time Labour had overtaken it as the main opposition to the Conservatives.

- Meanwhile, the Conservatives revived, entering the government in 1915.

- Labour began to create a distinctive image after Henderson broke away from Lloyd George's war cabinet.

- An important development affecting all the parties was the **Representation of the People Act** (1918), by which the vote was given to men over 21 and women over 30.

The government

- Lloyd George reorganised the government. He set up a small **war cabinet** of five men and a Cabinet Secretariat to co-ordinate the different departments.

- Government controls were set up over merchant shipping, farming and factories, and the coal mines were put under direct government management.

- **Conscription** was introduced in 1916, and food rationing in 1918.

Examiner's Tip

The most important political effects of the war were the split in the Liberal Party, which was a main reason for the rise of Labour in the 1920s, and the increased role of the state in people's lives.

Votes for women

The status of women

- The status of women in the mid-nineteenth century was that of second-class citizens. Working-class women often worked long hours for low wages, but middle-class women were not expected to have careers. Women were barred from the universities and the professions. When they married, their property passed to their husbands. They were not allowed to vote or to become MPs.

- In the second half of the century, things began very slowly to improve. Girls' schools and women's colleges at Oxford and Cambridge were founded. Increasing numbers of women went into teaching as a career. A few began to qualify as doctors. The Married Women's Property Act (1882) gave them the legal right to own their own property.

Suffragists and suffragettes

- During the 1860s a number of women's suffrage societies were formed in various parts of the country. In 1897, Millicent Fawcett formed the National Union of Women's Suffrage Societies to co-ordinate their work. The members of the NUWSS were known as **suffragists**.

- In 1903 **Mrs Pankhurst**, together with her daughters Christabel and Sylvia, founded the Women's Social and Political Union (**suffragettes**). The Pankhursts advocated more militant tactics to draw attention to their demands.

The suffragette campaign

- Both political parties were divided on the issue, but the Liberals were generally more sympathetic than the Conservatives.

- The question was complicated by the fact that only 60 per cent of men had the vote. If the vote were given to all women, they would outnumber men. But only a minority of MPs was prepared to give the vote to all men and women.

- Several attempts were made between 1907 and 1912 to get a Bill through the House of Commons, but without government backing none succeeded.

- The suffragettes became increasingly **militant**, breaking windows and chaining themselves to the railings of Buckingham Palace. When imprisoned, suffragettes went on hunger strike.

- The suffragettes' tactics had some success at first. They gained much publicity and ensured that the issue had to be faced. By 1912 even Asquith accepted that women must be given the vote.

- The extremism of 1912–13 made the cabinet reluctant to proceed because they did not want to be seen to give in to violence. They countered the suffragettes' violence with the **Cat and Mouse Act**.

- When war broke out, the suffragettes called off their campaign. Their contribution to the war effort played a vital part in winning votes for women in 1918, though only for women aged 30 and over.

Examiner's Tip

The suffragettes' campaign won valuable publicity, but in the end their militancy was probably counter-productive. The part women played in the war was the decisive factor in gaining them the vote.

The rise of the Labour Party

The 'New Model' trade unions

- The **Amalgamated Society of Engineers**, founded in 1851, was the first successful attempt to form a large-scale national trade union and it was followed by a number of other unions of skilled workers.
- These 'New Model' unions had high subscriptions from which they provided unemployment and sickness benefits. They tried to avoid strikes.
- In 1868 a number of union leaders (the 'Junta') set up the **Trades Union Congress**.
- In 1867 the case of *Hornby v. Close* presented them with a problem: the courts did not recognise their right to protect their funds.
- The **Trade Union Act** (1871) gave them the legal status to protect their funds in the court, but the **Criminal Law Amendment Act** made peaceful picketing illegal.
- The **Conspiracy and Protection of Property Act** (1875) legalised peaceful picketing. The Employers and Workmen Act (1876) made breach of contract by either employers or workers a civil offence; previously, it had been a criminal offence on the part of the worker and had been used against strikers.

'New Unionism'

- The key point in the rise of 'New Unionism' was the success of the **London dockers' strike** (1889) – a successful strike by unskilled workers.
- The 'New' unions had lower subscriptions and did not provide unemployment or sickness benefits. They tended to be more militant than the 'New Model' unions and many of their leaders were socialists.
- In the 1890s the growth of the 'New' unions was slow, mainly because of the economic depression.

The Taff Vale case

- In 1899 the *Lyons v. Wilkins* case cast doubt on the legality of peaceful picketing.
- In 1901 in the Taff Vale Case, the Amalgamated Society of Railway Servants was ordered to pay £23 000 damages, plus costs, to the Taff Vale Railway Company for losses suffered as a result of a strike. This ruling meant that strike action would bankrupt a union.
- The Taff Vale Case highlighted the need for parliamentary representation.

The origins of the Labour movement

- The origins of the Labour Party lie in the rise of a large and growing industrial working class.
- Skilled workers enjoyed a rising standard of living but around 30 per cent of the working class were living in severe poverty. Agricultural workers, too, often received starvation level wages.
- Awareness of these inequalities fuelled a demand, among both the working classes and middle-class intellectuals, for social reform.

(Continued next page)

The rise of the Labour Party

- Socialist ideas, such as those of Karl Marx, who spent half his life in London, had their impact. In 1884, two socialist societies, the **Social Democratic Federation** and the **Fabian Society**, were founded. Their members were largely middle class.
- The **Independent Labour Party** was formed in 1893 by **Keir Hardie** with the aim of securing the election of MPs who would represent the interests of 'labour', i.e. the working classes.
- The 1867 and 1884 Reform Acts enfranchised many working-class voters and a few working-class men were elected as 'Liberal-Labour' MPs. But the lack of social reform from both Gladstone's second ministry and Salisbury's ministries disappointed many working-class electors.

The formation of the Labour Representation Committee

- In the 1890s, trade union interest in political action began to develop. Many of the leaders of the 'New' unions were socialists and wanted political action to improve the condition of the poor.
- The failure of the engineers' strike in 1897–98 and the *Lyons v. Wilkins* case in 1899 convinced the TUC of the need for MPs to represent them in Parliament.
- In 1900, the TUC called a meeting in London which was attended by the SDF, the Fabians and the ILP. They agreed to set up the **Labour Representation Committee.** Its secretary was **Ramsay MacDonald**. Keir Hardie was one of two LRC candidates elected to parliament in 1900.
- At first, many trade union leaders were unenthusiastic, but the Taff Vale case changed their minds.
- Macdonald made an electoral pact with the Liberals in 1903 as a result of which 29 Labour MPs were elected in 1906. In that year, the name Labour Party was adopted.

The development of the Labour Party, 1906–18

- Labour supported the Liberal government which came into office in December 1905.
- It succeeded in persuading the Liberals to reverse the Taff Vale judgement by the **Trade Disputes Act** of 1906. This enabled the party to win further support from the unions, including in 1909 the mineworkers.
- The **Osborne judgement** (1909), which ruled that it was illegal for trade unions to charge a political levy, was a setback. Labour MPs depended on trade union support since MPs were not paid. In 1911, however, payment for MPs was introduced, and by the Trade Union Act of 1913 unions were allowed to charge a political levy, though members were allowed to contract out.
- Ramsay MacDonald, the Labour leader, opposed Britain's entry into the First World War and resigned the leadership. The new leader, Henderson, was a member of Asquith's coalition (1915–16) and Lloyd George's War Cabinet (1916) but resigned in 1917.
- To emphasise the distinctive nature of the Labour Party, Henderson gave Sidney Webb the task of producing a **Labour Manifesto**, which included a commitment to nationalisation (Clause 4).

Examiner's Tip

The Labour Party came into existence as a joint venture between the trade unions, the ILP and socialist societies with a largely middle-class membership.

Progress check

1. Why did nonconformists object to the 1902 Education Act?
2. What did Britain and France agree with each other in the Entente Cordiale?
3. What policy did Britain follow at the Algeciras Conference?
4. What was the effect of Chamberlain's tariff reform campaign on the Conservative Party?
5. How did New Liberalism differ from Gladstonian Liberalism?
6. What were the main provisions of the Children's Charter?
7. What was the purpose of the Trade Boards Act?
8. For whom were old age pensions provided in 1908?
9. How was the National Insurance scheme of 1911 financed?
10. What were the most controversial aspects of Lloyd George's 1909 budget?
11. How were the powers of the House of Lords defined by the Parliament Act of 1911?
12. What was the importance of the Parliament Act for Ireland?
13. What was the significance of the 'Curragh Mutiny'?
14. Why did Britain regard the German Naval Law of 1898 as particularly threatening to British interests?
15. What was agreed by the Anglo-French Naval Agreement of 1912?
16. What prompted Lloyd George to make his Mansion House speech threatening war against Germany in 1911?
17. How did Lloyd George as Prime Minister of the wartime coalition organise the government?
18. To whom was the vote given by the Representation of the People Act, 1918?
19. What was the importance of the Married Women's Property Act?
20. What was the difference between suffragists and suffragettes?
21. What was the Cat and Mouse Act?
22. What were the distinctive features of the 'New Model' trade unions?
23. What benefit did the trade unions gain from the Trade Union Act of 1871?
24. What was the significance of the dockers' strike of 1889 for the development of trade unions?
25. In what ways did the 'New' unions of the 1890s differ from the 'New Model' unions?
26. Who founded the Independent Labour Party and what was its aim?
27. How were trade unions affected by the Taff Vale judgement?
28. What was the significance of the Liberal-Labour Pact of 1904?
29. What rights did the Trade Union Act of 1913 confer on trade unions?
30. What was the importance of the Labour Manifesto of 1918?

Answers on page 89–90

The inter-war years

The Lloyd George coalition, 1918–22

The Coupon Election, 1918

- The wartime coalition, supported by the majority of the Conservative Party and the Lloyd George Liberals, fought the election as a coalition.
- Opponents of the coalition were the Asquith Liberals, the Labour Party and a few Conservatives.
- Lloyd George's popularity as the man who had led Britain to victory gave the coalition an overwhelming victory.

The economy and industrial relations

- The coalition tried to honour the promise that post-war Britain would be 'a land fit for heroes to live in' by **Addison's housing drive**, the Unemployment Insurance Act of 1920 and an increase in old age pensions.
- After a brief post-war boom, there was a slump in 1921. Unemployment rose to nearly two million and as a result, public expenditure rose.
- The government then made expenditure cuts (the **Geddes Axe**), mainly affecting the armed forces, education and housing. Addison's housing drive was abandoned.
- The Sankey Commission, appointed in 1919 to investigate the problems of the coal industry, failed to reach agreement. In 1921, the government handed the mines back to the owners, who immediately proposed wage cuts. The miners went on strike, but were defeated after the collapse of the Triple Alliance (**Black Friday**).

Ireland, 1916–22

- Sinn Fein triumphed in Ireland in the 1918 general election and set up an (illegal) Irish parliament in Dublin. A rebellion broke out, which the government tried to suppress with the **'Black and Tans'**.
- A 'treaty' was made with Sinn Fein in 1921. Most of Ireland was given dominion status, but Northern Ireland remained part of the United Kingdom, with a parliament for local affairs.
- The **Irish Free State** was set up in 1922, but there was then a civil war in Ireland.

The end of the coalition

- In 1922 the Conservatives withdrew from the coalition (Carlton Club meeting). They had become increasingly unhappy with Lloyd George as Prime Minister because he was a Liberal at the head of a mainly Conservative government.
- The Conservatives disliked the Irish treaty, which broke up the Union.
- They thought Lloyd George had handled the Chanak crisis badly.
- Lloyd George was criticised for selling honours to finance the Liberal party.

Examiner's Tip

Lloyd George held office after 1918 by courtesy of the Conservatives who used his popularity as the man who won the war to their own advantage and then cast him off when he no longer served their purpose.

The General Strike, 1926

Causes

- The coal industry was inefficient and in need of modernisation. The miners believed this could only be achieved by nationalisation, which the government rejected. The mines were under government control during the war but in 1921 Lloyd George handed them back to the owners.
- The problems of the industry worsened in the 1920s. In 1925, following the return to the gold standard and the ending of the Ruhr crisis, coal exports dropped. The coal owners proposed a wage cut, which the mine workers rejected.
- The government averted a strike by providing a subsidy and appointing the **Samuel Commission** to investigate the problems of the industry. When the commission reported, both sides rejected its proposals.
- A miners' strike followed, and the miners turned to the TUC for support. Mindful of the collapse of the Triple Alliance in 1921, the TUC ordered a general strike.

Why did the General Strike fail?

- The government had prepared emergency plans to safeguard food supplies and transport and to maintain order.
- The TUC had not made proper preparations for a general strike.
- Moderate leaders in the TUC began to fear that the strike might lead to violence and that they would lose control of it.
- They also realised that trade union funds were likely to run out.

Results

- Trade union membership dropped because workers were disillusioned with industrial action. Instead, they looked to parliament for improvements – hence the increase in Labour votes in the 1929 general election.
- The coal industry was not modernised and continued to decline.
- The government made general or sympathetic strikes illegal in the **Trade Disputes Act** (1927); this Act also hit Labour Party funding by making the political levy subject to **contracting in.**

Examiner's Tip

The government feared the revolutionary implications of a general strike, and the TUC came to think it had been playing with fire. Both were probably wrong about the risks of revolution.

The Labour Governments, 1924 and 1929–31

The first Labour ministry, 1924

- In the 1922 election, Labour gained more seats than the Liberals and became the **official opposition**.

- In 1923 it made further gains. The Conservatives, who had called the election to seek a mandate for tariff reform, lost their overall majority. MacDonald, as leader of the next largest party, was asked to form a **minority government** in January 1924.

- The main domestic achievements of the first Labour ministry were the Wheatley Housing Act and increases in unemployment benefits and old age pensions.

- In foreign affairs, MacDonald restored diplomatic relations with the USSR and played an important role in negotiating the Dawes Plan and the Geneva Protocol.

- However, the ministry depended on Liberal support, which it lost over the Campbell case. The subsequent general election was heavily influenced by the **Zinoviev letter**. It was probably a forgery but it caused great alarm. The Conservatives won a big majority.

The second Labour ministry (1929–31)

- In the general election of 1929, Labour emerged for the first time as the biggest party, though still without an overall majority.

- In domestic affairs it achieved little apart from a new Housing Act.

- In 1931 it was overtaken by a **financial crisis** resulting from the Great Depression. Unemployment had risen to 2.75 million, and as a result, expenditure on benefits went up, while the tax yield went down.

- The **May Committee** produced an alarming report in July 1931, which led to a run on the pound.

- The Chancellor of the Exchequer, Snowden, wanted to cut unemployment benefit to save the pound, as proposed by the May Committee, but the Cabinet could not agree on this and the Labour government resigned.

- To the surprise of his colleagues, MacDonald then accepted office as Prime Minister of a **National Government** to deal with the crisis. He was supported by the Conservatives and most of the Liberals, but only a few Labour MPs followed him.

- In the 1931 general election, the National Government won an overwhelming victory; Labour was reduced to 52 seats. The majority of the Labour Party condemned MacDonald.

Labour in the 1930s

- Labour swung to the left after the disaster of 1931. The new leader, **Lansbury**, was an idealistic socialist and a pacifist. He resigned in 1935 over rearmament and was succeeded by **Attlee**.

- There was much debate in the party among young left-wing intellectuals about socialist planning. Some, such as Cripps, wanted Labour to form a common front with the Communists.

- In the 1935 election, Labour won 154 seats – back to the position of 1924.

Examiner's Tip

MacDonald was accused of betraying the Labour Party in 1931, in the pursuit of personal ambition. But he may have believed that an all-party government was needed in the national interest to restore confidence.

Britain's inter-war economy

Britain's economic problems

- Unemployment never fell below one million between 1921 and 1939. The underlying cause was Britain's long-term economic decline, exacerbated by the war.
- The older export industries – coal, textiles, shipbuilding, iron and steel – suffered most. Consequently there was high unemployment throughout the period in the north of England, South Wales and Scotland.
- The Great Depression made the problem much worse. Unemployment reached over three millions in 1932–33.
- Governments followed a policy of deflation. Some alternatives were suggested but not adopted. J.M. **Keynes** argued for a programme of public works, which would create jobs and stimulate economic activity.

The National Government's economic policies

- The immediate financial crisis in 1931 was tackled by orthodox deflationary methods: 10 per cent cuts in public sector pay and unemployment benefit.
- The government was nevertheless forced to **abandon the gold standard** in 1931. This actually benefited British exports.
- In 1932 free trade was abandoned and **protective tariffs** were introduced. This increased the domestic market for British goods and brought in more revenue to the government.
- An attempt to set up a scheme of imperial preference at the **Ottawa Conference** of 1932 met with only limited success.
- An attempt was made to tackle the problem of the decline of the older industrial areas by the **Special Areas Act** (1934).

Economic recovery

- By 1933 the economy was recovering under the stimulus of the revival of world trade and a domestic housing boom.
- In the south and the midlands, the second half of the 1930s was a time of growing prosperity. New industries such as car manufacturing were expanding.
- The older industrial areas remained depressed.

The treatment of the unemployed

- In 1920 the original 1911 National Insurance scheme was extended to most workers with incomes below £250 a year, and benefits were increased.
- In 1921 'uncovenanted' benefit (**the dole**) was instituted.
- In 1931 because of the financial crisis, benefits were cut by 10 per cent and means testing was imposed for all those unemployed for more than six months.
- The 10 per cent cut was restored in 1934 when the Unemployment Assistance Board was set up to take over administration of the dole. The **Means Test**, which was applied to payments of the dole, was greatly resented.

> **Examiner's Tip**
>
> In spite of the relative prosperity of the midlands and south, the 1930s came to be remembered for the plight of the unemployed in the depressed areas. This played a large part in the Labour victory in 1945.

Britain and the Second World War

Appeasement

- Britain responded to the aggressive nationalism of Japan, Italy and Germany by pursuing a policy of **appeasement**. Unfortunately, each successive act of appeasement was taken as a sign of weakness and led to further aggression.
- Mussolini was allowed to get away with the invasion of Ethiopia but felt aggrieved that sanctions had been imposed. He responded by allying with Hitler. Meanwhile, Hitler was able to reoccupy the Rhineland unopposed.
- Appeasement of Hitler reached its climax in 1938. In March, Britain accepted the *Anschluss*. At the **Munich conference** in September, Chamberlain finally gave way to Hitler's demand for the Sudetenland.
- In March 1939 Hitler took over the rest of Czechoslovakia. Chamberlain changed his policy and offered guarantees to Poland.
- When Hitler invaded Poland in September 1939, Britain declared war.

Britain and the Second World War: Churchill's wartime coalition

- In May 1940 Chamberlain resigned and **Churchill** formed a wartime coalition government.
- Attlee, the leader of the Labour Party, was a member of the Cabinet and later Deputy Prime Minister. Several other Labour leaders gained experience as ministers during the war.
- Churchill's impact on the war effort was considerable. He contributed enormously to lifting the morale of the British people in the dark days of 1940–41.

Britain's relationship with the USA

- In 1940–41 Britain stood alone against Germany. The Battle of Britain (August–September 1940) saved Britain from invasion. The USA remained neutral.
- Britain's war effort depended heavily on buying goods from America. For this the **Lend-Lease** scheme, agreed in 1941, proved vital.
- In 1941 Hitler invaded Russia and at the end of the year he declared war on the USA. Thus from 1942, Hitler faced the **Grand Alliance**.
- As a member of the Grand Alliance, Britain appeared to have an equal role with the USA and the USSR. In reality it was the least powerful of the three.
- Churchill's personal relationship with Roosevelt and Stalin was important for the co-ordination of the war effort.
- At **Teheran** (November 1943), the three leaders agreed on the invasion of France in 1944.
- At **Yalta** (February 1945), they agreed on the division of Germany into zones of occupation.
- At **Potsdam** (July–August 1945), Churchill was replaced half-way through the conference by Attlee as a result of the 1945 general election. Truman, the new US President, shared British suspicions about Stalin. Some further details of the post-war treatment of Germany were agreed but otherwise there was deadlock.

Examiner's Tip

Britain emerged from the war clearly the junior partner in its relationship with the USA, and with its economy greatly weakened.

Progress check

1 Why is the general election of 1918 known as the 'coupon election'?

2 What was the Geddes Axe?

3 What happened on Black Friday, 1921?

4 What changes were made to the government of Ireland in 1922?

5 Why did the government set up the Samuel Commission in 1925?

6 What preparations did the government make to cope with a general strike?

7 What were the terms of the Trade Disputes Act of 1927?

8 What were the main domestic achievements of the first Labour ministry (1924)?

9 How did the Zinoviev letter influence the 1924 election?

10 Why did the second Labour ministry resign in 1931?

11 Why was MacDonald accused of betraying the Labour Party in 1931?

12 What was the effect on British trade of abandoning the gold standard in 1931?

13 What did the National Government hope would be the outcome of the Ottawa Conference of 1932?

14 What solution did J.M. Keynes propose for Britain's economic problems during the Great Depression?

15 Why was unemployment highest and most persistent in the North of England, South Wales and Scotland?

16 What was the purpose of the Special Areas Act of 1934?

17 What effect did Britain's policy of appeasement have on Hitler?

18 How did Labour benefit from membership of the wartime coalition?

19 What was the importance of Lend-Lease for Britain's war effort?

20 Who represented Britain at Potsdam and why?

Answers on page 90

THE INTER-WAR YEARS

Post-war Britain, 1945–64

Labour and the Welfare State

The 1945 election

- Labour won an overall majority of 146 – the first time it had won an outright majority in an election. This was in spite of the popularity of Churchill.
- The electors blamed the Conservatives for inadequate social policies and failures in foreign policy in the 1930s.
- Labour caught the mood of the time with its manifesto **'Let Us Face the Future'** There was a general desire for a government committed to building a better future.
- The role of the Labour leaders in the wartime coalition ensured that they could not be accused of inexperience.

The Welfare State

- Labour's social reforms were based on the **Beveridge Report** (1942), which had identified five evils: want, disease, ignorance, squalor and idleness.
- The **National Health Service Act** (1946) provided free medical care for the whole population. It was to be financed partly from National Insurance contributions but mainly from taxation.
- The **National Insurance Act** (1946) covered all adults and provided increased sickness and unemployment benefits, old age pensions, widows' and orphans' pensions, maternity allowances and death grants.
- The National Assistance Act (1948) provided benefits for those not covered by National Insurance.
- The National Insurance Industrial Injuries Act provided compensation for injuries and pensions for the disabled.
- In education the **Butler Act** of 1944 was carried out. Secondary education was provided for all children, and from 1947 the school leaving age was raised to 15.
- Over a million houses were built, but there was still a serious shortage in 1951.
- The **New Towns Act** (1946) aimed to create towns which were healthy and pleasant.
- The Town and Country Planning Act (1946) made county councils responsible for planning.
- The **Trade Disputes Act** (1946), though not strictly a welfare measure, reversed the Act of 1927. Trade unions were now able to levy a contribution for political purposes, provided that members were allowed to contract out of it.

Examiner's Tip

Labour's greatest achievement was to set up the welfare state it had promised. But it lost popularity because economic problems, controls, rationing and austerity continued.

Labour and the post-war economy

The economy

- In 1945 Britain had lost much of its export trade, faced a huge balance of payments deficit and had incurred massive debts, mainly to the USA. Moreover, the need to modernise industry was even greater than in the 1930s.

- Labour's policy for tackling these problems was a planned economy.

- A key part of this was **nationalisation**. Between 1945 and 1951, Labour nationalised the Bank of England, air transport, Cable and Wireless, the coal mines, the railways, docks, canals, road haulage, electricity and gas.

- It also nationalised iron and steel, but only after it had reduced the delaying powers of the Lords to one year by the **Parliament Act** of 1949.

- Labour relied heavily on government **controls**. Food rationing continued. Rents, profits, interest rates and foreign exchange were all controlled. There were strict building restrictions.

- Britain was helped through its immediate post-war difficulties by an **American loan** in 1946. This was given on condition that the pound sterling was made convertible. However, when this was put into effect in 1947, it led to a balance of payments crisis.

- **Cripps**, who became Chancellor of the Exchequer in 1947, believed that austerity was the solution to Britain's economic problems. He imposed import controls to direct economic activity towards exports.

- By 1950 exports were 75 per cent above the 1938 level. Even so, the balance of payments continued to be a problem and it was necessary in 1949 to devalue the pound.

Why did Labour lose the 1951 election?

- People were tired of **rationing**, austerity, controls and the continuing housing shortage. The Conservative manifesto offered to end all of these.

- The balance of payments deficit worsened in 1950–51 because the **Korean War** caused a sharp rise in the price of imported raw materials.

- The Korean War also made it necessary to increase the period of national service to two years, which was unpopular.

- The government faced financial problems resulting from the unexpectedly high cost of the National Health Service and the cost of the Korean War. The Chancellor, Gaitskell, tackled them by making expenditure cuts, and introducing charges for spectacles and dental treatment.

- This in turn led to the resignation of **Bevan** and **Wilson** from the government and a split in the party.

- The government seemed tired, especially in the period between the 1950 and 1951 elections when it had a very small majority.

- The Conservative Party had overhauled its organisation and its election campaign was much more effective.

- The Liberal Party had very little money for a second election in less than two years and put up very few candidates. This benefited the Conservatives.

Examiner's Tip

Labour carried out its promises on nationalisation, maintained full employment and led Britain to recovery after the war. But the performance of the economy remained a long-term problem.

Britain's position in the post-war world

- At the end of the war, Britain still had its empire and a worldwide military presence. As one of the 'big three' in the wartime Grand Alliance, it still aspired to a position as one of the world's leading powers.
- In reality, the post-war world was dominated by the two superpowers, the USA and the USSR. Britain's resources had been stretched to the limit by the war and it faced the problem of adjusting to a reduced role.

The retreat from Empire

- Before the war, Labour had produced plans for Britain to withdraw from India, and Indian nationalists expected a Labour government to grant independence.
- The problem was the religious division of India between Hindus and Muslims, which posed a serious risk of civil war.
- Mountbatten, who was sent to India as Viceroy in 1947, decided that partition was the only answer and that Britain should withdraw as quickly as possible.
- In 1947 the independent states of **India** and **Pakistan** came into being. There was widespread violence and huge numbers of refugees.
- Britain also withdrew from **Palestine,** which had been a British mandate since 1919. Unable to maintain order between Jewish settlers and the Palestinian Arabs, it handed the problem over to the United Nations in 1948.

Britain and the Cold War

- In 1944–45 Britain and the USA became increasingly suspicious of Russian intentions. By 1946, Communist governments had been established throughout Eastern Europe. Churchill was able to speak of an **Iron Curtain** across Europe.
- **Bevin** thought the best answer to this was Anglo-American co-operation.
- In 1947 he told the Americans that Britain could no longer afford to defend Greece against the Communists. President Truman's response was the **Truman Doctrine**, which committed the USA to defending non-communist Europe against Russia.
- In the **Marshall Plan** (1947), the United States offered American aid towards the economic recovery of Europe. Bevin took the lead in establishing the Organisation for European Economic Co-operation in 1948, to administer the scheme.
- He also played a key role in setting up the **Brussels Treaty** of 1948, a mutual defence pact between Britain, France and the Benelux countries.
- Britain and the USA worked closely together to overcome the **Berlin blockade** by the Air Lift (June 1948–May 1949). They then set up the Federal Republic in Western Germany in 1949.
- As a result of the Berlin blockade, and building upon the foundations of the Brussels Treaty, **NATO** was set up in 1949.
- The next major crisis of the cold war was the **Korean War**. Britain sent a contingent and embarked on a rearmament programme which posed considerable financial problems for the Labour Ministry in its last year.

Examiner's Tip

Bevin played a major role in engaging the USA in the defence of Western Europe, as the cold war developed. The setting up of NATO was his crowning achievement.

The Conservatives, 1951–64

Eden and Macmillan

- Churchill was 77 in 1951 and left much of the work to the Deputy Prime Minister, Eden, who succeeded him in 1955. Eden's ministry was cut short by illness and notable chiefly for the disastrous Suez campaign (1956).
- Macmillan (1957–63) was a 'one nation Tory', believing in social reform. He restored the Conservatives' confidence after Suez and led them to a third successive election victory in 1959.
- His ministry was marked by prosperity and rising standards of living but the underlying economic problems remained unsolved.
- Britain began to come to terms with its reduced influence in a world dominated by the superpowers, the USA and the USSR, and with the need to dismantle its empire.

Economic and social changes

- The 1950s were the years of the 'affluent society'. Living standards improved markedly. Wages rose faster than prices, and people were able to afford more consumer goods. Income tax was reduced. Unemployment was low.
- Food rationing and building restrictions were ended and controls swept away. National service was ended.
- A vigorous 'national housing crusade' by Macmillan as Minister of Housing produced a 50 per cent increase in the number of new houses.

Stop-go

- The economic policy of the Conservatives came to be called 'stop-go'. They tackled the balance of payments deficit by credit restrictions and import controls. When the balance of payments moved into surplus, they cut interest rates and taxes, which led to a period of boom, resulting in a renewed balance of payments deficit.
- The timing of the 'go' phases helped the Conservatives to win the elections of 1955 and 1959, but by the early 1960s it was becoming clear that the underlying growth of the economy was lagging behind Britain's European competitors.
- Some would argue that the Conservatives' failure to join the EEC when it was set up in 1957 was a crucial mistake.

The election of 1964

The Conservatives lost the election of 1964.

- The 'stop-go' economic cycle did not favour them.
- An application to join the EEC was vetoed by France in 1963.
- The government was damaged by the Profumo scandal.
- Some Conservatives opposed Macmillan's policy of granting independence to African colonies.
- Home, Macmillan's successor as Prime Minister in 1963, was an electoral liability.
- Labour's fortunes were reviving. Under the direction of Wilson, elected as Labour leader in 1963 on the death of Gaitskell, Labour presented a more dynamic image, offering encouragement of technological change and planning of the economy.

The economic policies of the Conservatives produced the 'affluent society' but no solution to Britain's long-term economic problems.

Progress check

1 What impact did the Labour manifesto ' Let Us Face the Future' have in the 1945 election?

2 What social problems did the Beveridge report identify?

3 How was the National Health Service financed?

4 What steps did Labour take to carry out the 1944 Education Act?

5 How successful was Labour in tackling the housing problem?

6 What change did Labour make to the powers of the House of Lords?

7 Which industries did Labour nationalise?

8 What condition was attached to the American loan of 1946 and what unfortunate effect did this have?

9 What effect did the Korean War have on Britain's economy?

10 Why did Bevan and Wilson resign from the Labour government in 1950?

11 What features of Labour's record in government were most unpopular by 1951?

12 Why was Britain's withdrawal from India accompanied by widespread violence?

13 What was the response of the USA to Britain's withdrawal of its troops from Greece?

14 What was the Marshall Plan?

15 What did Macmillan achieve as Minister of Housing?

16 What is meant by describing Macmillan as a 'one nation Tory'?

17 What is meant by 'stop-go'?

18 Why are the late 1950s and the early 1960s described as the period of the 'affluent society'?

19 Why did Britain's application to join the EEC in 1963 fail?

20 What did Labour offer voters in the 1964 election?

Answers on page 90

France, 1814–75

The restored Bourbons

Political divisions in nineteenth-century France

- The revolutionary period left France politically divided between republicans, Bonapartists and royalists.
- **Republicans** saw the monarchy as a symbol of a hated social and political system.
- **Bonapartism** was relatively weak after Waterloo, but it became a powerful element in French politics later in the century. Many Frenchmen began to look back to the greatness of France in the Napoleonic era.
- **Royalists** saw the return of the monarchy as offering stability against the possibility of revolution.

Louis XVIII, 1815–24

- Louis XVIII was restored by the victorious allies. He was, therefore, to many Frenchmen the symbol of defeat in the Napoleonic Wars.
- Realising that the monarchy must win the loyalty of the French nation, he issued the **Charter** in 1814. He promised to rule as a constitutional monarch in co-operation with an Assembly elected on a narrow middle-class franchise.
- In 1815 the **'Ultras'** won a majority in the Assembly and proceeded to carry out a purge of the Bonapartists (the **'White Terror'**). Louis realised that this was a mistake and checked it by appointing new ministers.
- In 1820, after the **murder of the Duc de Berry**, the Ultras were able to persuade him to reduce some of the freedoms granted in the Charter, especially freedom of the press.

Charles X, 1824–30

- Charles X ordered compensation to be paid to *émigré* nobles who had lost their estates during the Revolution.
- The religious ceremonies on which he insisted at his coronation, alarmed anti-clericals who were further upset when the Church was given control over education. Press censorship was tightened.
- In 1829 he appointed one of the most extreme of the Ultras, **Polignac**, as his chief minister. The result was a clash with the Chamber of Deputies.
- Polignac then issued the reactionary **Ordinances of St Cloud**, which virtually destroyed the Charter of 1814.
- In July 1830 **revolution** erupted and Charles was overthrown.

Examiner's Tip

Louis XVIII tried to heal the divisions in post-Napoleonic France but Charles X followed right-wing policies which seemed to be an attempt to restore the ancien regime.

The Orleans monarchy and the 1848 revolution

Louis Philippe

- As a result of the revolution of 1830, Louis Philippe was offered the crown by the Chamber of Deputies. Thus he was in effect an **elected** king.

- Despite his aristocratic origins, Louis Philippe was a **typical bourgeois** in his habits. He seemed the ideal choice. As a member of the royal family he was acceptable to royalists, yet moderate republicans also approved of him because he was willing to accept the role of a constitutional monarch.

- The constitution was based on the Charter of 1814. Electoral power was in the hands of the middle classes.

- There was rapid **industrial development** in some areas of France.

- The benefits of economic growth were not felt by the working classes. The government was unwilling to interfere in the economy by introducing social reforms.

- The combination of social unrest and the French revolutionary tradition caused sporadic outbreaks of violence. The worst of these were risings in Paris and Lyons in 1834, which were brutally suppressed.

- Louis Philippe avoided an adventurous foreign policy because of the expense of war and because he was uncertain whether his regime enjoyed sufficient support to take the risk. His critics accused him and **Guizot**, his Foreign Minister from 1840 to 1847, of subservience to Britain.

The growth of opposition

- Economic hardship and the lack of social reform caused working-class discontent.

- A new revolutionary movement grew up, led by **Louis Blanc**, an early socialist who preached the **'right to work'**.

- The king's advisers, such as Guizot, were anti-liberal and the regime became corrupt and inefficient.

- Louis Napoleon exploited the mood of disillusion to revive support for Bonapartism.

The 1848 Revolution

- Discontent focused on the demand for extension of the franchise. In February 1848, revolution broke out when Guizot banned a 'reform banquet' in Paris. On February 24, Louis Philippe was forced to abdicate.

- A provisional government was set up which included radicals and the socialist Louis Blanc. **'National Workshops'** for the unemployed were set up in Paris.

- In May, the radicals and socialists were excluded from the government. The National Workshops were closed and Louis Blanc fled.

- This provoked a desperate uprising in Paris – the **'June Days'**. General Cavaignac turned the guns on the rebels and hundreds were massacred.

- In December, Louis Napoleon was elected President by an overwhelming majority.

Examiner's Tip

Napoleon triumphed because his name was a symbol of France's past glories, he offered stability against the 'red peril' which had arisen in the June Days, and his schemes for social reform won working-class support.

Napoleon III: The Second Republic and the Second Empire

The Second Republic

- Under the constitution, Napoleon was President for four years only and not allowed to seek re-election. He was not prepared to accept this, so he set out to make himself popular.

- He opposed demands by republicans in the Assembly to reduce the electorate.

- He won support from the Catholics by sending troops to Rome to overthrow the Roman Republic and restore the Pope.

- In December 1851 he carried out a coup d'état and declared himself President for ten years. Many of his political opponents were exiled to Algeria.

- In 1852 he abolished the Second Republic and made himself the Emperor Napoleon III. Both these steps were approved by plebiscites.

The consolidation of the Second Empire

- Under the constitution, Napoleon III had autocratic powers. His rule was based on popular approval through plebiscites. He appointed ministers, controlled foreign policy and the armed forces, and initiated legislation.

- The Legislative Assembly had little power. In any case, the elections were managed.

- There was strict press censorship. Political associations were suppressed.

The 'Liberal Empire'

- In 1859 Napoleon granted an amnesty to political opponents exiled in 1851.

- In 1860 he began to liberalise the Second Empire. The Legislative Assembly was given the right to debate its reply to the address from the throne, and the press was allowed to report parliamentary debates.

- During the 1860s press censorship was relaxed and opposition journals and newspapers sprang up. Trade unions were legalised. It became increasingly accepted for ministers to be questioned in parliament.

- In 1869–70 a new constitution gave the Legislative Assembly the power to propose laws and vote on the budget. A ministry representing the majority in the Legislative Assembly was formed in January 1870. These changes are known as the 'Liberal Empire'.

Social and economic developments

- The Second Empire saw considerable economic growth. New banks were founded to raise capital for commercial and industrial development. Low interest rates encouraged investment. The railway network was vastly increased and mining and heavy industry were expanded. Public works helped to create full employment.

- A great deal of slum clearance was undertaken in Paris and new boulevards and squares were created under the guidance of Baron Haussmann.

Examiner's Tip

Historians debate whether the move to the 'Liberal Empire' sprang from a genuine desire to liberalise the constitution or was forced on Napoleon by a succession of failures in foreign policy.

Napoleon III: foreign affairs and downfall

Foreign Policy

- Napoleon wanted – and was expected – to restore to France the glory it had had in his uncle's day.
- France and its allies were victorious in the **Crimean War** of 1854–56, though the French army did not earn the glory Napoleon had hoped. The fact that the peace conference was held in Paris gave the Second Empire prestige.
- In 1859 in alliance with Piedmont, he went to **war against Austria**. After winning victories at Magenta and Solferino, he made the **Truce of Villafranca**.
- The episode aroused opposition from both Catholics and liberals. Catholics feared for the papacy and liberals felt that Napoleon had let the Italians down.
- He lost prestige by the ill-considered **Mexican adventure** of 1861–67.
- In 1866 he was persuaded by Bismarck to remain neutral while Prussia defeated Austria. Prussia's victory left France facing a much more powerful Prussia.
- Napoleon's unsuccessful attempt to restore the balance of power by trying to annex Luxemburg as compensation, discredited him further.

The Franco-Prussian War

- Napoleon tried to use the issue of the **Hohenzollern candidature** for the Spanish throne to score a diplomatic victory over Prussia and thus restore his prestige. This provided Bismarck with the opportunity to provoke a war by editing and publishing the **Ems Telegram**. Napoleon gave way to French public opinion and declared war.
- The French armies were unprepared for war and were disastrously defeated at **Metz** and **Sedan**. The Second Empire was overthrown and a republic set up.
- Paris fell after a four-month siege in January 1871.
- By the Treaty of Frankfurt, France was forced to surrender **Alsace and Lorraine**, to accept an army of occupation and to pay an indemnity.

The Establishment of the Third Republic

- The new republic was challenged by the **Paris Commune** in March–May 1871. The immediate cause was the Assembly's decision at the end of the siege that payment of rents must be resumed.
- **Thiers**, head of the government, ordered the army to suppress the Commune. There was much brutality and the episode left deep divisions in French society.
- Thiers played a leading role in raising the money to pay the indemnity, and in 1873 the army of occupation was withdrawn.
- Royalists had a majority in the Assembly but were divided between the supporters of the Comte de Chambord (Bourbon) and the Comte de Paris (Orleanist).
- Since they were unable to agree who should be king, the Assembly in 1875 accepted a republican constitution, with a President as head of state.

Examiner's Tip

Napoleon's considerable domestic successes were outweighed by foreign policy failures. As he had enjoyed full power in France, he was held responsible for the disaster of 1870.

Progress check

1 What did Louis XVIII promise in the Charter of 1814?

2 What were the aims of the 'Ultras'?

3 What was the White Terror?

4 How did the murder of the Duc de Berry affect French politics?

5 What was the importance of the form of coronation adopted by Charles X?

6 What were the Ordinances of St Cloud?

7 Why was Louis Philippe known as the 'Citizen King'?

8 What policies were advocated by Louis Blanc?

9 On what grounds was Louis Philippe's foreign policy criticised?

10 Why was Guizot unpopular?

11 What were the 'June Days' and how did they help Louis Napoleon to gain election as President of the Second Republic?

12 What political benefit did Louis Napoleon derive from sending troops to Rome in 1849?

13 What powers did Napoleon III have as Emperor?

14 What constitutional changes were made in setting up the 'Liberal Empire' in 1869–70?

15 For what is Baron Haussmann famous?

16 Why were Napoleon III's policies towards Italy in 1859–60 disapproved of by (a) the Catholics and (b) the Liberals?

17 In what way was the outcome of the Austro-Prussian war of 1867 contrary to French interests?

18 Why did Napoleon oppose the Hohenzollern candidature for the Spanish throne?

19 What terms did France have to accept in the Treaty of Frankfurt?

20 What was the greatest weakness of the royalists in the early 1870s?

Answers on page 91

Russia, 1825–1917

Tsarist Russia, 1825–55

The Tsarist autocracy

- Early nineteenth-century Russia was perhaps the most reactionary state in Europe.
- The system of government by a Tsar with absolute authority was an **autocracy**.
- Russia's social structure was distinguished by the survival of **serfdom,** which had disappeared everywhere else in Europe. The majority of Russians were serfs, owned either by the crown or by the landed aristocracy.
- The middle class was tiny, reflecting the lack of industry and the relative unimportance of trade in Russia's backward economy.
- The **Orthodox Church** had a central role in society and the state, and acted as a brake on change.

The Decembrist movement

- Even in Russia, liberal ideas had penetrated among some of the educated nobles.
- When Alexander I died in December 1825, the throne was vacant for three weeks and the liberals rose up, demanding a national assembly. The new Tsar, Nicholas I, suppressed the revolt with great severity.

Nicholas I, 1825–1855

- Nicholas followed a policy of **repression** based on the army and the police – particularly the 'Third Section' or secret police.
- In Poland there was a revolt in 1830, which was crushed. Poland was placed under military rule and Polish nationalism was suppressed.
- The backwardness and inefficiency of Russia were highlighted by defeat in the Crimean War (1854–56).

Examiner's Tip

Nicholas I's repression preserved the autocracy, the aristocracy and the Orthodox Church from change, but it also left Russia stagnating.

Alexander II and Alexander III, 1855–94

The emancipation of the serfs, 1861

- The peasants were freed from all their obligations to the landlords. The government compensated the landlords and reclaimed the money from the peasants by redemption payments over a period of 49 years.

- The land was not transferred to individuals but to the '*mir*' or village commune, which was collectively responsible for the redemption payments. For this reason it was very difficult for peasants to leave the village.

- The peasants got the poorer land and their holdings were small. Since the land was communally owned and regularly redistributed, there was no incentive to improve it. Russian agriculture therefore remained backward and inefficient.

Alexander II's other reforms

- In 1864 'zemstva' (elected district councils) were set up. Although the electoral system favoured the nobility and gentry, they were a step towards democracy.

- Legal reforms were introduced, including trials in public, trial by jury and salaries for judges (to reduce bribery).

- The army was reformed. Conscription played an important part in reducing illiteracy, since conscripts were taught to read and write.

- There was also some economic development. A State Bank was set up, railways were built and there was some industrial development.

Renewed repression

- After 1866 Alexander's regime became more repressive. The powers of the 'zemstva' were reduced. Press censorship was strict, the secret police were active and political cases were tried without a jury.

Revolutionary movements

- Many intellectuals, desperately aware of Russia's backwardness, formed reformist movements. Repression turned some of them into revolutionary movements.

- The two most important were the Narodniki, who wanted to educate the peasants to demand reforms, and the anarchists, led by Bakunin, who called for armed rebellion. Anarchists made several attempts on the life of Alexander II. They succeeded in 1881.

Alexander III, 1881–94

- The keynote of the reign of Alexander III was repression, enforced by his chief minister, Pobedonostsev. The Okhrana (secret police) were active. There was strict press censorship. The 'zemstva' were put under the supervision of Land Captains.

- Anti-semitism was encouraged. Pogroms (armed attacks on Jews) were common.

- Industrialisation increased. Work began on the Trans-Siberian Railway. In 1892, Alexander appointed Witte as Minister of Finance.

- In foreign relations in 1893, Russia allied with France.

Examiner's Tip

The emancipation of the serfs was the most important change in Russia in the nineteenth century, but it created almost as many problems as it solved.

Nicholas II and the 1905 Revolution

Economic advance

- The state took the key role in promoting economic development. Witte was successful in encouraging foreign investment, especially from France.
- The rail network more than doubled between 1890 and 1914. The rate of growth of industrial production was the highest in the world.
- The urban population grew rapidly, especially in Moscow and St. Petersburg where housing and working conditions were appalling.

Political developments

- Nicholas II continued the repressive policies of Alexander III, but reformist and revolutionary movements continued to develop.
- In 1898 the Marxist **Social Democratic Party** was founded by Plekhanov. At its 1903 Congress, held in exile in Brussels and London, it divided into two wings. The **Bolsheviks**, led by Lenin, wanted membership restricted to a small number of dedicated activists. The **Mensheviks** wanted a mass party of the working class.
- In 1902 the **Social Revolutionary Party** was formed. This aimed to bring about revolution by propaganda and terror.
- In 1904 the **Liberals** set up the Union of Liberation.

The 1905 Revolution

- Discontent boiled over into revolution as a result of the **Russo-Japanese War** (1904–05). The Russian government expected 'a short victorious war that would stem the tide of revolution', but the Japanese won handsomely.
- News of defeat in the Far East brought discontent to a head on January 22, 1905, when several hundred peaceful, unarmed demonstrators carrying a petition to the Tsar were killed on **Bloody Sunday.**
- This provoked a wave of strikes and peasant uprisings. In June there was a mutiny on the battleship **Potemkin** and in September a general strike.
- In St Petersburg a **Soviet** was set up with Trotsky as co-chairman.
- The Tsar was forced to make concessions. In August he promised to set up a **Duma**.
- In October he issued a manifesto promising a wider franchise and legislative powers for the Duma. This satisfied the Liberals and divided them from the workers in the Soviet.
- The government was then able to suppress the revolution. The leaders of the Soviet were arrested and a rising in Moscow was brutally suppressed.

Why did the Revolution of 1905 fail?

- The revolutionaries were not united, so eventually the Tsar was able to split the Liberals from the Socialists.
- There was no central leadership.
- Lenin and other revolutionary leaders were in exile abroad and arrived too late.
- At the critical moment, the Tsar made concessions in the **October Manifesto**
- The army and navy for the most part remained loyal.

Examiner's Tip

Tsarist Russia was shaken by the 1905 Revolution but recovered. However, it never fully regained the loyalty it lost on Bloody Sunday.

Nicholas II: from revolution to war

1905–14: The Dumas and Stolypin

Nicholas II believed in autocracy and saw political concessions as weakness. He had no intention of observing the spirit of the October Manifesto.

- The First Duma met in May 1906. The electoral system was rigged to favour the landowners and middle classes. Nicholas dissolved it after ten weeks because the Cadets (Liberals) demanded reforms which he was not prepared to grant.

- The Second Duma (1907) was also soon dissolved because its demands were unacceptable to Nicholas.

- The Third Duma (1907–12) and the Fourth Duma (1912–17) were elected on a revised franchise, which increased still further the power of the gentry and middle classes. They were dominated by Octobrists (moderate liberals) and achieved some modest reforms.

Stolypin

- In 1906 Stolypin replaced Witte, whom Nicholas blamed for having forced him to issue the October Manifesto.

- He introduced important agrarian reforms. Redemption payments were ended. Peasants were given complete freedom to leave the 'mir' and they were allowed to turn their holdings into their own individual properties.

- Stolypin hoped that this would create a class of prosperous peasant farmers and would make agriculture more efficient.

Russia in 1914

There were indications that Tsarist Russia might survive:

- The Third and Fourth Dumas co-operated with the government and could have been the foundation for a gradual development of democracy.

- A class of prosperous peasants was slowly beginning to emerge.

- There were some signs of improvement in the conditions of industrial workers.

- Industrial output was growing, especially in coal and iron; other industries were slower to grow.

But Russia still faced serious problems:

- The regime was still autocratic and repressive.

- The reputation of the monarchy never fully recovered from Bloody Sunday.

- Industry was still small in scale and inefficient by western European standards.

- Agricultural productivity was still poor despite Stolypin's reforms, which in any case needed many years to have a real effect.

- Nicholas II lacked the intelligence to deal with his problems. He failed to acknowledge the need for change and did not realise how much prestige the monarchy had lost in 1905. The growing influence of Rasputin further discredited the court.

- His advisers were mediocre. Only two had real ability – Witte, who was dismissed in 1906, and Stolypin, who was assassinated in 1911.

Examiner's Tip

Since 1890, Russia had made enormous progress economically and some progress politically, but it was ill-equipped to face the strains of the First World War.

The 1917 Revolutions

The First World War

- The war exposed Russia's inefficiency. Losses were enormous. Millions of men were drafted into the armed forces but the Russian state was unable to provide them with adequate clothing, training or equipment.
- Crushing defeats were suffered at Tannenberg and the Masurian Lakes in 1914. In 1915, the Russians were driven out of Poland. In 1916, an offensive against Austria met with some success – but then equipment began to run short. Since the Tsar had decided to take personal command of the army, the defeats were blamed on him.
- The government became increasingly unstable. In the first two years of the war, there were four prime ministers. The Tsar was absent at army headquarters. Continuity was provided only by the Tsarina Alexandra and her favourite, Rasputin.
- Food became increasingly difficult to obtain in the towns and prices rose.

The February Revolution

- On 23 February 1917 (Russian calendar), a wave of strikes and food riots broke out, particularly in Petrograd. Troops sent to quell the rioters joined them. The authority of the government had collapsed.
- In Petrograd, the Soviet of Workers' and Soldiers' Deputies was set up.
- On 1 March, the Fourth Duma established a Provisional Government under the Liberal Prince Lvov. The next day the Tsar abdicated.

The Provisional Government

- The Provisional Government never enjoyed much support. It made the mistake of continuing the war, which led to further defeats and continuing food shortages.
- A disastrous offensive in Galicia in July provoked an abortive rising in Petrograd.
- As a result Prince Lvov was replaced by a Social Revolutionary, Kerensky.
- Rumours began to spread that land was to be redistributed, so the peasants in the army deserted.
- An attempted right-wing coup by General Kornilov was defeated, but only with the help of the Bolsheviks.

Lenin and the October Revolution

- In April, Lenin returned to Russia. In the 'April Theses' he set out his aim, 'all power to the soviets'. This meant overthrowing the Provisional Government.
- In July, the Bolsheviks made a premature attempt to seize power.
- Lenin then fled to Finland and many of his followers were arrested.
- On his return he played a key role in persuading the Bolshevik Central Committee to organise an armed insurrection.
- The revolution took place on the night of 6–7 November (October 24–25 by Russian dating). The next day, the All-Russian Congress of Soviets confirmed the Bolsheviks in power.

Examiner's Tip

The October Revolution was a coup by a determined minority. The Bolsheviks took advantage of the weakness of the Provisional Government, which had failed to address Russia's problems.

Progress check

1 What was the aim of the Decembrist movement?

2 What was the 'Third Section'?

3 How was Poland treated after the revolution of 1830?

4 Why was it difficult for peasants to leave the village after the emancipation of the serfs?

5 What were the zemstva and how were they elected?

6 What legal reforms were introduced by Alexander II?

7 What were the Narodniki?

8 Explain (a) Okhrana; (b) pogrom.

9 What was the importance of the 1903 Congress of the Social Democratic Party?

10 What was the immediate cause of the 1905 Revolution?

11 What happened on Bloody Sunday?

12 What did the Tsar promise in the October Manifesto?

13 Why did Nicholas II dissolve the First Duma?

14 What was the dominant group in the Third and Fourth Dumas?

15 Why did Nicholas II dismiss Witte?

16 What did Stolypin hope to achieve by his agrarian reforms?

17 Name the two battles in which the Russians suffered heavy losses in 1914.

18 What was the importance of the April Theses?

19 Why did the Russian army suffer massive desertions in 1917?

20 Who were (a) Prince Lvov; (b) Kornilov?

Answers on page 91

The unification of Italy

The Risorgimento

Italy before 1848

- In 1815 Italy was divided up into a number of states. It was dominated by Austria and its Chancellor, Metternich. Lombardy and Venetia were part of the Austrian Empire. Most of the other Italian states looked to Austria for protection.
- Only Piedmont-Sardinia was independent of Austrian influence.

The growth of liberal and nationalist ideas

- Secret societies, the most famous of which was the Carbonari, were formed.
- Three possible national leaders emerged. Mazzini, who founded 'Young Italy' in 1831, aimed to make Italy 'united, independent and free'. He believed the Italians could do this by their own efforts.
- Charles Albert, who became King of Piedmont in 1831, aimed to create a kingdom in northern Italy rather than to unite the whole peninsula.
- Pius IX, who became Pope in 1846, had the reputation of being a liberal. For many Italians the papacy was the natural focus of leadership. Some, for example Gioberti, aimed for a confederation of Italian states under the papacy.

The 1848 Revolutions

- Revolts in Sicily and Naples in January 1848 forced King Ferdinand to set up a constitutional government and touched off a series of uprisings.
- Charles Albert and Pius IX granted constitutions in Piedmont and Rome.
- Revolts in Milan and Venice expelled the Austrians.
- Charles Albert declared war on Austria but was defeated at the battles of Custozza (1848) and Novara (1849). In 1849, he abdicated in favour of Victor Emmanuel II. The Austrian general, Radetzky, regained control of Milan.
- In Rome, Pius IX fled and Mazzini set up the Roman Republic. French troops eventually restored the Pope, despite heroic resistance led by Garibaldi.
- In Naples, King Ferdinand dismissed his liberal government and restored his autocracy by bombarding Sicily into submission.
- Finally, in August 1849, Austria regained control of Venice.

Reasons for the failure of the 1848 Revolutions

- The Italians could not defeat Austrian military power unaided.
- The Italian revolutionaries were divided over their aims. Mazzini aimed for a republic, Charles Albert for a monarchy (of northern Italy only).
- Many Italians gave higher priority to setting up constitutional government in the separate states than to a unified Italy.

Examiner's Tip

1848 was an important step towards unification but it also demonstrated that allies would be needed to overcome Austria.

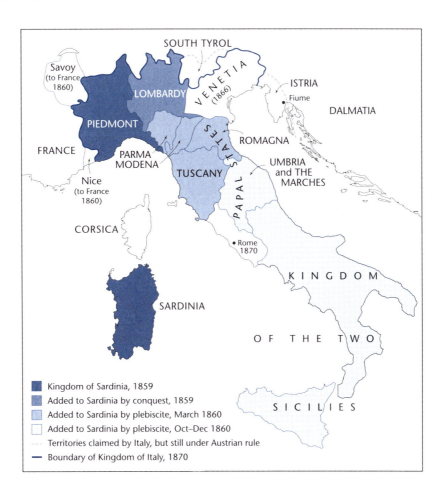

Cavour and Piedmont

- By 1849 Piedmont under its new king, Victor Emmanuel II, was the focus of nationalist hopes.

- **Cavour**, who was appointed Prime Minister in 1852, aimed to build up Piedmont's strength. His reforms improved communications, expanded trade and strengthened finance.

- Cavour also realised that Piedmont would need a powerful ally against Austria. He sought the friendship of Napoleon III of France. Piedmont's participation in the Crimean War as an ally of France and Britain helped.

- In 1858 he made the **Pact of Plombières** with Napoleon III.

The unification of northern Italy

- In 1859 the Franco-Piedmontese armies occupied Lombardy, defeating the Austrians at **Magenta** and **Solferino**.

- Napoleon then made peace (the **Truce of Villafranca**), leaving Venetia in Austrian hands.

- The war inspired rebellions in other parts of northern Italy and this enabled Cavour to use plebiscites to join **Parma, Modena, Tuscany and the Romagna** to Piedmont and Lombardy in a new kingdom in northern Italy in 1860.

(Continued next page)

The process of unification, 1859–71

Garibaldi's expedition to Sicily and Naples

- In 1860 Garibaldi collected a force of a thousand volunteers, sailed from Genoa to Sicily and quickly gained control over the whole island.
- In August he crossed to the mainland and in September he captured Naples. He then intended to march on Rome.
- Cavour was worried that, if Garibaldi attacked Rome, the Catholic powers of Europe might intervene. He therefore sent troops into the Papal States from the north. The Italian army occupied the Marches and Umbria but kept well clear of Rome itself.
- This army then linked up with Garibaldi, who handed over his conquests to Victor Emmanuel.
- In January 1861 the first all-Italian parliament met in Turin. Less than six months later, Cavour died.

Venice and Rome

- Venetia became part of Italy in 1866, as a by-product of the Seven Weeks' War in which Italy fought against Austria as the ally of Prussia.
- In Rome, the Pope had the protection of French troops. Consequently, two attempts by Garibaldi in 1862 and 1867 to occupy Rome were unsuccessful.
- In 1870 French troops were withdrawn from Rome because of the Franco-Prussian War. Rome was then occupied by Italian troops and became the capital.
- The Pope refused to recognise this and became a virtual prisoner in the Vatican until an agreement was made with Mussolini in 1929.

The Kingdom of Italy

- The system of government of Italy after unification was a constitutional monarchy under Victor Emmanuel II of Piedmont.
- The ministers were responsible to a parliament elected on a rather narrow middle-class franchise. This system survived for over half a century, but eventually it failed to give effective government and gave way to the dictatorship of Mussolini.
- Economic development was slow. This was partly because Italy lacked coal and iron. Industry did develop in the north, but Italy remained comparatively poor. Extreme poverty and ignorance in the south remained one of Italy's most serious social problems.

Examiner's Tip

Cavour was the main architect of Italian unification but he was forced to modify his plans by Garibaldi. The result was an Italy ruled by a monarchy, as Cavour wished, but lacking real unity.

Progress check

1 Which was the only Italian state independent of Austrian influence after 1815?

2 What was the Carbonari?

3 What was the aim of Young Italy and who was its leader?

4 What was the aim of Charles Albert of Piedmont?

5 Why did many Italians look to Pope Pius IX as a national leader?

6 What was the aim of Gioberti?

7 Where did the 1848 Revolutions in Italy begin?

8 What was the main reason for the downfall of the Roman Republic in 1849?

9 What was the outcome of the war between Piedmont and Austria in 1848–49?

10 What lesson did Cavour draw from the defeat of Piedmont in the war against Austria in 1848?

11 Why did Piedmont take part in the Crimean War?

12 What was the Pact of Plombières?

13 What was the Truce of Villafranca?

14 Which states joined the Kingdom of Northern Italy as a result of plebiscites in 1860?

15 Why was Cavour alarmed by Garibaldi's successes in Sicily and Naples?

16 How did he respond to Garibaldi's successes?

17 How did Venetia become part of the Kingdom of Italy?

18 Why was it not possible to make Rome part of a united Italy in the 1860s?

19 What made it possible to bring Rome into the Kingdom of Italy in 1870?

20 What form of government was adopted for the Kingdom of Italy?

Answers on page 92

The unification of Germany

Germany, 1815–62

The German Confederation

- In 1815 Germany was divided into 39 separate states, which formed the German Confederation.
- The Bundestag (Federal Assembly) consisted of representatives of the governments of the states and was no more than a co-ordinating body. It was presided over by Austria and from 1815 to 1848 was effectively run by the Austrian Chancellor, Metternich, who used it repress liberals.
- The two biggest states by far were Austria and Prussia, both of which also ruled territories outside the borders of the Confederation.

The 1848 Revolution and the Frankfurt Parliament

- In 1848 there were revolutions throughout Germany. These led to the election of a parliament for the whole of Germany, the Frankfurt Parliament of 1848–49. Its members were largely middle-class liberals who aimed to draw up a constitution for a united Germany.
- Its members were divided between those who argued for a Little Germany (Kleindeutschland), which would exclude Austria, and those who wanted a Great Germany (Grossdeutschland) including the Austrian lands except Hungary.
- Both the Austrian Emperor and the King of Prussia turned down the crown of a federal Germany. The Parliament broke up in 1849.
- In 1850, in the Submission of Olmütz, Frederick William IV of Prussia acknowledged Austria's revival of the Confederation.

The Zollverein and the growth of the Prussian economy

- Free trade was established in Prussia 1821. This led to the creation in 1834 of the Zollverein (customs union), which established free trade throughout most of Germany except Austria.
- The development of heavy industry and the railway network gave Prussia economic predominance and helped Roon and William I to develop Prussia's military strength.
- The Zollverein and the economic strength of Prussia laid the foundation for the unification of Germany under Prussia.

Examiner's Tip

The 1848 Revolutions left many Germans disillusioned with liberalism: the attempt to set up a united Germany by constitutional means had failed.

Bismarck

The appointment of Bismarck as Prime Minister of Prussia

- The cost of Roon's plans to expand the army led to a crisis between the King and the Prussian Parliament.
- In 1862 William I appointed Bismarck as Prime Minister. He was appointed because of his reputation for strong anti-liberal views.
- Bismarck simply collected the taxes needed to enlarge the army, even though the parliament refused to approve them.

The Danish War, 1864

- Christian IX of Denmark, who succeeded to the throne in 1863, wanted to make Schleswig part of Denmark.
- Bismarck took the opportunity to present himself as the champion of German interests. In co-operation with Austria, he made war on Denmark, which was quickly defeated.
- By the Convention of Gastein (1865), Prussia took Schleswig, and Austria, Holstein. This gave Bismarck the chance to pick a quarrel with Austria whenever he liked.

The Austrian War (The Seven Weeks' War), 1866

- Bismarck next planned a war against Austria. He made an alliance with Italy, which wanted Venetia. At a meeting with Napoleon III at Biarritz he made vague promises of future compensation for France.
- In 1866, he provoked war by proposing that the German Confederation should be dissolved and a new confederation set up excluding Austria. The main Austrian army was overwhelmingly defeated at Sadowa in Bohemia.

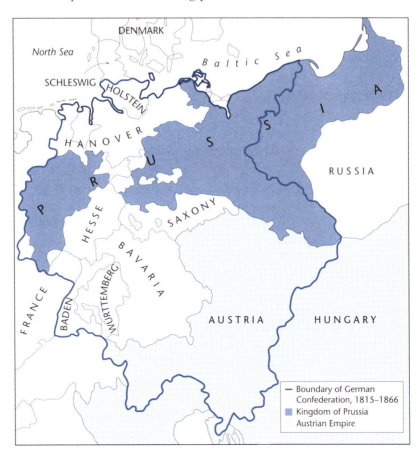

(Continued next page)

Bismarck

- By the Treaty of Prague, the German Confederation was abolished and a new North German Confederation was set up. The south German states were to be independent.
- Schleswig-Holstein was handed over to Prussia and soon afterwards Prussia annexed Hanover and several other north German states.

The Franco-Prussian War, 1870–71

- After 1866 it became increasingly difficult to avoid a war against France. Public opinion in France regarded the defeat of Austria by Prussia as a defeat for France. Prussia's gains in the war were greatly resented.
- Bismarck's disclosure that Napoleon had asked for compensation in the Rhineland or Belgium inflamed relations further.
- Matters came to a head in 1870 over the issue of the succession to the Spanish throne. Napoleon III demanded that Prince Leopold of Hohenzollern should withdraw his candidature. This was agreed, but Napoleon then demanded guarantees that the candidature would not be renewed.
- It was clear that he was seeking a diplomatic victory at Prussia's expense. Bismarck altered the telegram in which William announced his rejection of the latest French demands (the Ems Telegram) so that the French government could only take it as a rebuff. Public opinion in Paris was outraged and demanded war.
- The French were unable to find allies as Bismarck's diplomacy had kept Napoleon isolated.
- The Prussian armies triumphed at Metz and Sedan and went on to capture Paris after a four-month siege.
- In January an armistice was signed and in May 1871 peace was made at Frankfurt. Alsace and Lorraine became part of Germany and France was to pay an indemnity and accept the occupation of its northern provinces.

The establishment of the German Empire

- The war enabled Bismarck to complete the unification of Germany. The southern states of Bavaria, Baden and Württemberg were swept into a unified Germany. The new Empire excluded Austria.

Why was Bismarck successful in uniting Germany?

- Prussian military power overcame the hostility of Austria and France. Thus the roles of Roon and Moltke in building up the Prussian army were crucial.
- The economic development of Prussia underlay its military power. The economic and military strength of Prussia enabled Bismarck to achieve political unification.
- Bismarck's own contribution through his cynical and unscrupulous diplomacy was vital. His deception of Napoleon III at Biarritz kept Austria isolated in 1866. His lenient treatment of Austria after the Seven Weeks' War kept Austria neutral in the Franco-Prussian War.
- He kept Britain neutral in 1870 by revealing that Napoleon III had had his eye on Belgium in 1866 as 'compensation' for Prussia's gains in the Seven Weeks' War.
- He encouraged Russia to take advantage of France's involvement in war to repudiate the Black Sea clauses of the Treaty of Paris of 1856.

Examiner's Tip

Some historians believe that Bismarck planned his wars with unification as his goal, but most argue that he simply aimed to extend Prussia's power and took advantage of events as they happened.

The German Empire, 1871–90

The Imperial Constitution

- The new German Empire (the Second Reich) was a **federal** state.
- William I of Prussia as Emperor (**Kaiser**) was head of the executive and the army. He had the right to declare war or martial law in an emergency.
- The **Chancellor** (Bismarck) was appointed by and responsible to the Emperor, with whom power ultimately lay.
- The **Bundesrat** (upper house of parliament) consisted of representatives of the German states. Prussia, the biggest state, had the most representatives. As Minister President of Prussia, Bismarck was therefore able to control the Bundesrat.
- The lower house (**Reichstag**) was elected by universal male suffrage and this made the constitution appear unusually democratic for its time.
- However, the Reichstag had no control over the Chancellor and could not secure his dismissal. Its powers were limited to a veto over legislation and control over the federal budget.

Bismarck and the Liberals

- At first, Bismarck relied on the Liberals for a majority in the Reichstag, partly because he needed their support in his quarrel with the Catholics.
- In 1874 he quarrelled with them over the size of the army, which accounted for 90 per cent of the federal budget.
- The decisive break came in 1879 when **tariffs** were introduced. Henceforth, he relied on the Conservatives and the Catholic Centre Party in the Reichstag. This was a turning point in his relations with the political parties.

The Kulturkampf

- Bismarck feared that the loyalty of German Catholics to Rome would conflict with their loyalty to the Empire. The growth of ultramontanism, highlighted by the doctrine of papal infallibility in 1870, strengthened his suspicions.
- By the **May Laws** of 1873–75, education was brought under state control and state approval was required for the licensing of priests.
- The campaign backfired. The Catholic Centre Party made gains in the Reichstag elections of 1877. Since Bismarck needed their support against the Liberals over tariffs, he toned down the Kulturkampf and withdrew some of the May Laws.

The Socialists

- In 1875 the Social Democratic Party was founded on the basis of the Gotha Programme. In 1877, the party won half a million votes in the Reichstag election.
- In 1878 Bismarck introduced the **anti-Socialist laws** which banned Socialist organisations, meetings and newspapers. The Socialists were not, however, banned from membership of the Reichstag and the party continued to grow in strength.
- He also introduced **'state socialism'** (sickness and accident insurance and old age pensions). The aim was to undermine support for the Socialists.

Examiner's Tip

Although he quarrelled with the Catholics, the Liberals and the Socialists, Bismarck gave Germany an era of great stability, in which its industrial power grew rapidly.

THE UNIFICATION OF GERMANY

Bismarck's foreign policy, 1871–90

Foreign affairs

The main aim of Bismarck's foreign policy after 1871 was to keep the peace. This meant keeping France isolated and cultivating good relations with both Austria-Hungary and Russia.

- The **Balkan crisis** of 1875–78 presented a major threat to peace. Bismarck feared that it could lead to a war between Russia and Austria-Hungary. He therefore called the **Congress of Berlin** and, acting as 'honest broker', worked out a settlement which reduced the size of the Russian-dominated Bulgaria which had been created at the end of the Russo-Turkish War of 1877–78. This reassured Austria.

- In the Congress of Berlin, Bismarck had backed Austria, but this created the risk of driving Russia into an alliance with France.

Over the next years he created a complex web of agreements to deal with this problem:

- 1879, the **Dual Alliance** with Austria – a secret defensive alliance which was the cornerstone of German diplomacy until 1918.

- 1881, the **Dreikaiserbund** (League of Three Emperors) – a looser agreement with Austria and Russia in which all three promised not to help a fourth power (presumably France) in a war against one of the others. The agreement was renewed in 1884 but lapsed in 1887.

- 1882, the **Triple Alliance** – a defensive alliance with Austria and Italy.

- 1887, the **Reinsurance Treaty** with Russia. Germany and Russia promised to remain neutral in a war involving the other unless Germany attacked France or Russia attacked Austria-Hungary.

Colonies

- Bismarck was reluctant to get involved in the race for colonies, but eventually he had to yield to pressure from industrialists and nationalists.

- In 1884–85, he called the **Berlin Conference** at which the European powers in effect agreed to carve up Africa among themselves.

- Germany acquired colonies in South West Africa, East Africa, Togoland and the Cameroons.

Examiner's Tip

Bismarck's diplomacy was extremely skilful but the system was so complex that it could not last. The conflicting interests of Austria and Russia made it impossible in the long term to preserve an alliance system involving both.

Germany under William II

The economy

- In the period after 1870, Germany's economy developed very rapidly, so that by 1914 its industrial strength rivalled, and in some spheres overtook, that of Britain.
- Industrialisation was accompanied by urbanisation. Germany's population increased rapidly and there was considerable internal migration from the countryside to the towns.
- Migrants to the towns were attracted by the hope of employment and higher wages. Nevertheless, many found themselves living in slums, working long hours in poor conditions and liable to periodic unemployment.
- The rise of the Socialist Party was closely linked to the growth of an urban proletariat.
- At the same time, the development of large-scale industrial concerns led to the rise of an industrial élite with considerable political influence but with interests which sometimes conflicted with those of the older agrarian élite (e.g. over tariffs and protection).

The structure of politics: the Reichstag and the political parties

- The Reichstag did not have the power to remove the Chancellor, nor did the defeat of a government measure in the Reichstag force him to resign. It did, however, have the power to veto legislation and it controlled the non-military part of the imperial budget.
- The Chancellor therefore needed to try to gain the support of enough parties or groups to approve his policies. The divisions in German society, reflected in the Reichstag, made this difficult.
- The most notable development in the Reichstag in the reign of William II was the steady rise of the **Socialist Party**. By 1912 it was the biggest party.
- The **Conservatives** lost ground in the 1890s to small right-wing, anti-Semitic parties, and responded by adopting anti-Semitic policies themselves, along with strong support for protection of agriculture.
- Other groups with a significant presence in the Reichstag were the Catholic Centre Party and the Liberals (divided into National Liberals and Progressives).

Pressure groups

Pressure groups played an important part in politics:

- The **Pan-German League** (founded 1891) built up support for William II's Weltpolitik.
- The **Navy League** (1898) campaigned for Tirpitz's programme of naval expansion.
- The **Army League** (1912) pressed the Reichstag to pass the army bills of 1912–13.
- The **Agrarian League** (1893) campaigned for protection for agriculture. Its success in mobilising peasant discontent played an important part in the radicalisation of the Conservative Party.

(Continued next page)

Germany under William II

The political élites

Much political influence was wielded by three powerful interest groups:

- Agrarian interests. Because Prussia was the largest state, the Prussian **Junkers** (landed gentry) had disproportionate political influence in the Bundesrat. They used their power to block political reform and to protect the interests of agriculture.

- Industrialists. Industrialisation led to the emergence of a powerful and wealthy group of big **industrialists**. They supported William II's Weltpolitik and provided the finance for the Pan-German League and the Navy League. They supported Tirpitz's plans for expansion of the navy. Opposition to Socialism united the industrialists and the landowners. But there were also tensions between industrial and agrarian interests over the issue of protection.

- The army. William took his role as head of the army very seriously. Some historians claim that the army leaders, and especially **Moltke**, the Chief of the General Staff, had more influence than the Chancellor in 1914.

Kaiser William II

- William II, who succeeded as Kaiser at the age of 29 in 1888, was neurotic and unpredictable. He was convinced of Germany's world-historic mission.

- He was an **autocrat** at the head of an autocratic system and he was determined to use his powers personally. As he was also head of the army, his personal power was very considerable.

- He disagreed with Bismarck about the anti-Socialist policies, colonial expansion and relations with Russia. In 1890, Bismarck retired 'because of his health'.

German Chancellors, 1890–1914

- **Caprivi** (1890–94) shared William II's views on the anti-Socialist laws and the alliance with Russia, both of which were allowed to lapse. Social welfare laws were passed. He was forced to resign when William became alarmed by growing support for the Socialist Party.

- Prince **Hohenlohe** (1894–1900) was an elderly and rather weak Chancellor. The real power lay with the Kaiser. From 1897, he often by-passed Hohenlohe and gave his confidence to Bülow (Foreign Secretary) and **Tirpitz** (Secretary for the Navy).

- **Bülow** (1900–09) pursued a policy of 'social imperialism', appealing to nationalistic fervour and enthusiasm for the naval building programme. His parliamentary support, the 'Bülow bloc', broke up over his tax proposals to meet the growing budget deficit in 1908. At the same time, William II's '*Daily Telegraph*' interview led to an open rift between the Kaiser and the Chancellor, who resigned in 1909.

- **Bethmann-Hollweg** (1909–17) faced continued financial crisis, though he was able to secure the passing of the army bills in 1912–13. When the Socialists emerged as the largest party in the Reichstag in 1912, it became increasingly difficult to achieve stable parliamentary majorities. The Chancellor was therefore dependent on the emperor and the army. This was the situation in the crisis of 1914.

Examiner's Tip

Power lay with the agrarian and industrial élites, the army and the bureaucracy. Chancellors had to manoeuvre between the Kaiser, the political parties in the Reichstag, the élites and the army.

William II and the coming of the First World War

William II's foreign policy

- William abandoned Bismarck's policy of keeping on good terms with both Austria and Russia. The Reinsurance Treaty with Russia was not renewed in 1890 and by 1893 Russia and France had formed an alliance. Thus the isolation of France, which Bismarck had seen as vital to Germany's security, ended.

- At the heart of William's foreign policy was his *Weltpolitik* (world policy). In practice this meant gaining colonies, building up the navy and extending German influence in the Balkans.

Anglo-German relations, 1904–14

- In the 1890s, it seemed likely that if Britain sought an ally it would be Germany.

- Relations began to deteriorate as a result of William's telegram to President **Kruger** of the Transvaal on the defeat of the Jameson Raid in 1896, and the anti-British attitude of the German press during the Boer War.

- A number of approaches by Britain were rebuffed, the last one in 1901. Britain therefore sought other allies. In 1902, it made an alliance with Japan, and in 1904 an entente with France.

- William next tried to undermine the Anglo-French Entente by visiting **Tangier** and demanding a conference on the future of Morocco. When it met at **Algeciras** in 1906, only Austria supported Germany. Germany's clumsy diplomacy strengthened the Anglo-French Entente.

- In 1907 the Anglo-Russian Entente completed the Triple Entente.

- In 1908 William II's *Daily Telegraph* interview antagonised British opinion.

- The second Morocco crisis (1911), when the German gunboat 'Panther' was sent to **Agadir**, provoked Lloyd George to threaten war. Germany backed down, though with some 'compensation' in the Congo.

The naval race

- The German **Naval Laws** (1898 and 1900) began the naval race between Germany and Britain.

- The race accelerated after 1906 when the *Dreadnought* was launched, and continued unabated up to the outbreak of war.

- British attempts to slow down the race (Haldane's mission to Berlin in 1912 and Churchill's suggestion of a 'naval holiday' in 1913) were unsuccessful.

- In 1912 Britain made the **Anglo-French Naval Agreement**.

The Balkans

- Bismarck had no ambition to expand German influence in the Balkans but he was concerned about the danger of war between Austria and Russia. This led to the formation in 1879 of the Dual Alliance with Austria, which was the cornerstone of German foreign policy from 1879 to 1914.

- In William II's reign, Germany's growing economic penetration of the Balkans produced a conflict of interest between Germany and Russia.

- In 1908 Austria annexed **Bosnia**. Serbia was outraged and turned to Russia for help. Russia was unable to do anything since William made it clear that Germany would back Austria in the event of war. Russia was snubbed and Serbia became a bitter enemy of Austria.

(Continued next page)

William II and the coming of the First World War

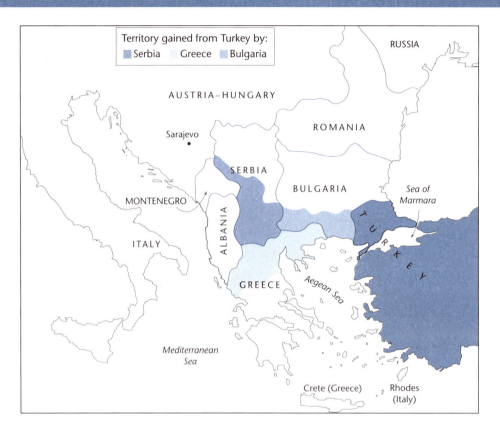

Territory gained from Turkey by:
- Serbia
- Greece
- Bulgaria

The Balkan Wars, 1912–13

- The Balkan Wars threatened to draw in Russia and Austria and cause a general war. Germany and Britain co-operated at the London peace conference to prevent this.
- Serbia was substantially enlarged by the wars but it was thwarted in its desire to gain access to the sea through Albania, mainly because Austria opposed this and was backed by Germany.
- Austria feared that a strengthened Serbia would attack Bosnia. This might herald the break-up of the multi-national Austrian Empire. Austria was therefore determined to crush Serbia. The assassination of Franz Ferdinand at Sarajevo provided the excuse.
- Austria consulted Germany before issuing an ultimatum. The Kaiser and the army leaders held strongly nationalistic and militaristic opinions, and they seem to have thought that a war was inevitable. William gave the Austrian chancellor a 'blank cheque' – a promise of German help without conditions.

The crisis of 1914

- On 28 July, Austria declared war on Serbia, even though Serbia accepted most of the terms of its ultimatum. Russia mobilised in support of Serbia.
- Germany declared war on Russia, then on France.
- German troops invaded Belgium in accordance with the Schlieffen Plan.
- Britain declared war on Germany.

Examiner's Tip

Germany must bear a considerable share of responsibility for the war. The army leaders had more control over policy than the Chancellor. There is some evidence that they were planning for war from 1912 onwards.

Progress check

1 Why did some members of the Frankfurt Parliament want to exclude Austria from a united Germany?

2 What was the outcome of the submission of Olmütz?

3 What was the Zollverein?

4 Why did William I appoint Bismarck as Prime Minister of Prussia in 1862?

5 What were the main differences between the German Confederation of 1815 and the North German Confederation of 1867?

6 What purpose did the Ems telegram serve for Bismarck?

7 What were the main terms of the Treaty of Frankfurt?

8 How did Bismarck ensure Britain's neutrality in the Franco-Prussian War?

9 What was the importance of Roon and Moltke in the unification of Germany?

10 To whom was the Chancellor responsible under the constitution of the German Empire, and why was this important?

11 What powers did the Reichstag have?

12 Over what issues did Bismarck fall out with the Liberals in the 1870s?

13 What was 'state socialism'?

14 With which powers did Bismarck wish to maintain good relations and which power did he wish to keep isolated?

15 What danger to German interests did he see in the Balkan Crisis of 1875–88?

16 Which powers formed the Triple Alliance and which were members of the Dreikaiserbund?

17 What were the main aims of (a) the Pan-German League and (b) the Agrarian League?

18 Who were the Junkers, and why did they have considerable political power in Wilhelmine Germany?

19 On what issues did William II disagree with Bismarck?

20 Who were the four German Chancellors between 1890 and 1914?

21 What was William II's *Weltpolitik*?

22 What did William II hope to gain from the Algeciras Conference, and what did he in fact achieve?

23 For what purpose did Tirpitz argue that Germany needed to expand its navy?

24 Why was Serbia disappointed with the outcome of the First Balkan War, despite gaining substantial additional territory?

25 What was meant by saying that Germany gave Austria a 'blank cheque' in 1914?

Answers on page 92

Italy, 1919–45

The rise of Fascism

The First World War and the peace treaty

- Italy's military record in the war was mixed. The Italians were badly beaten at **Caporetto** (1917), but they defeated the Austrians at **Vittorio Veneto** (1918).
- The Italians were bitterly disappointed by the peace settlement. They gained South Tyrol, Trentino, Trieste and part of Istria but their other claims were rejected. Particularly galling was the failure to get **Fiume**.

The economy

- The Italian economy was weak. Industrial development was slow and agriculture was backward.
- The war made matters worse: the total cost was enormous and Italy had to borrow heavily from the USA.
- Inflation during the war virtually wiped out the savings of the middle classes.
- Demobilisation and the end of wartime production led to high unemployment. Many unemployed ex-servicemen joined para-military organisations.

The political system

- Parliamentary democracy was discredited. Before the war, governments managed parliament by a system of bribery and corruption called **'transformism'**.
- **Regional differences**, particularly between the north and the south, were strong and worked against the growth of truly national parties.
- Disagreements about entering the war inflamed political divisions.
- The two largest parties, the Socialists and the Catholic Popular Party, were unable to co-operate and it was therefore impossible to form stable ministries. Between 1918 and 1922 there were five different governments.
- Many Italians thought Italy needed strong government more than democracy.

Mussolini's rise to power

- Italy was in chaos between 1918 and 1922. Strikes, riots and lawlessness became widespread and there were fears of a Communist revolution.
- The anti-Communists formed armed bands, of which the most important were the **Fasci di combattimento** (fighting groups) formed in Milan in 1919 by Mussolini.
- In 1921 he founded the National Fascist Party, which won 35 seats in the election.
- A **general strike** in 1922 provided him with the chance to gain power. The Fascists helped to defeat the strike while the government stood by, apparently helpless.
- In October 1922 Mussolini organised the **'march on Rome'**. The Prime Minister wanted to use the army and police to disperse the Fascists but King Victor Emmanuel III refused and instead invited Mussolini to form a government.

Examiner's Tip

Mussolini was invited to take office merely because he threatened to use force. At the time the Fascists had only 35 MPs.

The establishment of the Fascist dictatorship

The consolidation of Mussolini's power, 1922–25

- Mussolini formed a coalition with only four Fascists in the government. But he also persuaded Parliament to grant him dictatorial powers for a year.
- In 1923, a new Electoral Law (the **Acerbo Law**) provided that the party that gained most votes in a general election should have two-thirds of the seats in the Chamber of Deputies. In the 1924 election, the Fascists and their allies easily achieved this.
- The murder of **Matteotti**, who had publicly blamed Mussolini for violence during the election campaign, caused a parliamentary crisis. Opposition members left parliament (the **Aventine Secession**), leaving Mussolini in complete control.
- In 1925, he established himself as **dictator.** All other parties were banned, non-fascists removed from the government and opposition newspapers taken over.
- In December 1925, Mussolini became responsible to the King and not to Parliament, and at the same time the King's right to appoint or dismiss ministers was taken away.

Why was Mussolini able to establish a Fascist dictatorship?

- The most important reason was the virtual breakdown of parliamentary government. No stable government could be formed.
- Prime Ministers between 1918 and 1922 came to rely on the Fascist para-military bands as a counterweight to left-wing para-militaries.
- Giolitti, the Liberal Prime Minister in 1921–22, included the Fascists in his list of government candidates in the 1921 election, with the result that 35 Fascists were elected.

Support for the Fascists

Mussolini won the backing of important groups in Italian society:

- Landowners welcomed Fascist attacks on leagues of farm workers.
- Industrialists similarly welcomed their attacks on the trade unions.
- The middle classes feared a Communist revolution.
- The Catholic Church saw a Communist revolution as a major threat.
- The King helped to bring him to power by refusing to allow the army to be used against him.

Fascist ideas

Mussolini's main aim was simply to get power. Fascism had no coherent philosophy, but it did have some basic ideas.

- It stood for **strong, centralised government** and the subordination of the interests of the individual to the state. It emphasised national pride.
- It emphasised **leadership**: fascist propaganda depicted Mussolini as a hero.
- It was anti-democratic (hence a one-party state) and anti-Communist.
- It aimed for economic self-sufficiency (**autarchy**).

Examiner's Tip

Do not under-estimate the role of Mussolini himself. Not only did he found the Fascist Party but he also provided leadership. He had considerable political skills.

Mussolini's Italy

The Fascist state

- At the heart of the Fascist state was Mussolini – *Il Duce* (the leader). Mass rallies were organised to glorify him, and the media were used for propaganda. As dictator, he alone appointed ministers and he had the power to make laws by decree.

- The electoral system was changed in 1928 so that electors could only accept (or, in theory, reject) a list of candidates drawn up by the Fascist Grand Council.

- The Grand Council was the centrepiece of Mussolini's **Corporate State**. It consisted of representatives from each of the corporations set up by Mussolini to organise workers and employers.

- In 1938 the **Chamber of Fasces and Corporations** replaced the Chamber of Deputies (Parliament). It had little real power, however. It only met when Mussolini summoned it, and he played off its members against one another.

- Mussolini set up a secret police and the Special Tribunal for the Defence of the State, but they were less active and less ruthless than similar institutions in other dictatorships.

- Much of the existing machinery of government remained in operation. Local administration was still in the hands of the prefects. The monarchy, the army and the police were little changed.

The control of opinion

- Much effort was devoted to developing the **cult of the *Duce*** through the media. Newspapers and books were censored and the radio was state-controlled. The government tried to regulate the film industry to serve its propaganda purposes.

- The **Ministry of Popular Culture** tried to impose its ideas of Fascist culture in literature, music and art.

- Education was closely supervised. University teachers had to take an oath of loyalty to Mussolini. Schoolteachers had to be party members. Textbooks were re-written. Nevertheless, criticism of the regime in the universities was not totally suppressed.

- The indoctrination of the young was also pursued through Fascist youth groups.

Church and State

- One of Mussolini's successes was the **Lateran Treaty** (1929), by which he recognised the Vatican City as a sovereign state. Catholicism was recognised as the official state religion.

Examiner's Tip

Mussolini's Italy was a totalitarian state but his dictatorship was less repressive and less efficient than those of Germany and the USSR.

The economy and society

The Corporate State

- The Corporate State was the central feature of Mussolini's economic policy.
- Corporations were set up for each industry or occupation. They replaced trade unions, which were abolished, and consisted of representatives of employers and workers.
- The aim was to replace the capitalist system, in which employers and labour were often in conflict, with a system of co-operation. Strikes were therefore forbidden and the corporations were empowered to draw up labour contracts and settle labour disputes. It was, however, an inefficient system and favoured the employers.
- In 1938 the system was tied into the political structure when the Chamber of Deputies was replaced by a Chamber of Fasces and Corporations.

Economic policies

- **Public works** schemes were introduced to reduce unemployment. But many were not completed and a lot of money disappeared through corruption.
- Government **subsidies** were provided for industry. In 1933 the **IRI** (Institute for Industrial Reconstruction) was set up. Industrial production increased, but Italy still remained industrially weaker than the other European great powers.
- A programme of land reclamation was started, notably the draining of the **Pontine Marshes** near Rome.
- In the **'Battle for Grain'**, farmers were subsidised to produce more wheat. Wheat production doubled between 1922 and 1939. But to achieve this, land which was better suited to dairy or fruit farming was given over to wheat.
- Mussolini regarded maintaining the value of the lira as a matter of national prestige. Unfortunately, it was revalued at too high a level in 1926 and this led to a loss of exports. Wages had to be cut as a result. The Depression made matters worse. In 1936 Mussolini finally accepted a devaluation.
- Mussolini believed that a strong Italy needed a bigger population. Large families were encouraged by payment of child benefits, and bachelors faced extra taxation. In spite of this, the birth rate fell.

The social effects of Fascist policies

- Industrialists benefited from the Corporate State and from government subsidies.
- Landowners were helped by policies which made it difficult for agricultural workers to leave the land and therefore kept agricultural wages down.
- Many of the middle classes benefited from the expansion of the civil service. Those working in private enterprises, however, did not do so well.
- Industrial workers were worse off. Real wages declined, food prices rose and there was high unemployment, especially in the 1930s.
- Agricultural workers suffered a fall in real wages of up to 40 per cent in the 1930s.
- The working classes benefited from improved welfare provision. Pensions and unemployment benefits were increased.
- Women suffered a loss of status. Because of Mussolini's obsession with raising the

Examiner's Tip

The Italian economy remained comparatively weak in the 1930s. It was slow to recover from the Great Depression.

Foreign affairs

Foreign policy, 1922–35

- Fascism was **nationalistic** and aimed to make Italy great.
- Mussolini had an early success in the **Corfu Incident** (1923).
- In 1924 he gained further prestige in Italy by seizing **Fiume**.
- His foreign policy over the next ten years was mainly directed towards counteracting French influence in Eastern Europe and especially Yugoslavia. In the process he made Albania virtually an Italian protectorate.
- When Nazis tried to seize control in Austria in 1934 and murdered the Chancellor, Dollfuss, Mussolini moved troops to the Austrian frontier. Hitler abandoned his plans to unite Austria with Germany. This success boosted Mussolini's prestige.
- In 1935 he joined Britain and France in the **Stresa Front** to condemn German rearmament.

The Ethiopian War

- In 1935 Mussolini invaded **Ethiopia**. He saw the conquest of Ethiopia as the answer to Italy's economic problems and as a way of boosting his regime at a time when unrest was growing because of the effects of the Great Depression.
- The League of Nations declared Italy an aggressor and imposed **sanctions**, but coal, steel and – most importantly – **oil** were excluded. This was because Britain and France were anxious to maintain good relations with Italy.
- The Italian armies had little trouble in completing the conquest of Ethiopia.
- The mild sanctions which had been applied angered Mussolini. He withdrew from the League and drew closer to Germany.

Mussolini and Hitler, 1936–45

- Between 1936 and 1939, Mussolini's relations with Hitler became closer. In 1936, they reached an understanding (the **Rome-Berlin Axis**) and in 1937 Italy joined Germany and Japan in the Anti-Comintern Pact.
- Both Italy and Germany gave military assistance to Franco in the **Spanish Civil War**. Italy's contribution was a serious drain on its military resources.
- Mussolini accepted the Anschluss (March 1938), reversing the policy he had pursued in 1934. This damaged his prestige in Italy.
- His role at the **Munich Conference** in September 1938, when he seemed to have played a key part, revived his popularity a little.
- In April 1939 Mussolini sent troops into **Albania**. This was unnecessary as Italy already had economic control over Albania.
- Although Mussolini made the '**Pact of Steel**' with Hitler in May 1939, he stayed out of the Second World War in September.
- Italy entered the war in June 1940. The war was a disaster for Italy and led to the **overthrow of Mussolini** in 1943.
- He was then captured by the Germans and set up as the head of a puppet government in northern Italy. He was captured and executed by Italian partisans in 1945.

Examiner's Tip

Mussolini found it difficult to play second fiddle to Hitler. For this reason he went to war in 1940 knowing that Italy could not sustain a prolonged war. He was therefore directly responsible for Italy's defeat.

Progress check

1   What territorial gains did Italy make at the end of the First World War?

2   In what way did the peace settlement disappoint Italians?

3   What was 'transformism'?

4   What were the *fasci di combattimento?*

5   What was the Acerbo Law?

6   What was the importance of the murder of Matteotti?

7   What was the Aventine Secession? How did it help Mussolini?

8   Why did the Catholic Church support Mussolini despite his earlier atheist views?

9   Who were the members of the Fascist Grand Council?

10 What was agreed by the Lateran Treaty of 1929?

11 In what way did Mussolini claim that the Corporate State was better than the capitalist system?

12 What main criticism can be made of Mussolini's 'Battle for Grain'?

13 Why was Mussolini's determination to defend the lira bad for Italy's economy?

14 How did industrialists benefit from Mussolini's regime?

15 What were the benefits and disadvantages for the working classes of Mussolini's regime?

16 What did Mussolini gain from the Corfu Incident?

17 What was the Stresa Front?

18 Why were the sanctions imposed on Italy when it invaded Ethiopia, ineffective?

19 What was Mussolini's response to the imposition of sanctions?

20 What was Mussolini's attitude towards the Anschluss, and why did it harm his prestige?

Answers on page 93

Germany, 1918–45

The Weimar Republic

The November Revolution

- In November 1918 the German Empire collapsed in defeat. The German armies on the Western Front could no longer prevent the allied forces advancing into Germany. Germany asked for an **armistice**.
- When the armistice was signed, the German armies were still in France and the people did not realise how desperate the military situation was.
- The Kaiser abdicated and a provisional government was set up under a Social Democrat, **Ebert**.
- In January 1919 a National Assembly was elected which met at Weimar and drew up a new constitution.

The Weimar Constitution

- The **President** was elected by the people for a term of office of seven years. His most important function was to appoint the Chancellor, but he also had emergency powers to suspend the constitution and rule by **decree**.
- The **Chancellor** was normally the leader of the largest party in the Reichstag.
- The **Reichstag**, elected every four years by universal suffrage and proportional representation, controlled taxation and legislation.
- The Reichsrat consisted of representatives of the provinces and had only limited delaying powers.
- The constitution was **highly democratic**. Its weakness lay in the system of proportional representation.

The Treaty of Versailles

The provisional government only accepted the Treaty of Versailles with great reluctance when it realised that there was no alternative. The treaty was bitterly resented by most Germans because of:

- the way it was drawn up (the **diktat**);
- the extensive losses of territory (14 per cent of Germany's land area and all its colonies);
- the heavy **reparations** (fixed in 1921 at £6600 million);
- the severe limits on the size of the armed forces;
- most of all, the **'War Guilt' clause**.

Challenges from Right and Left

- At the end of the war, the Communists hoped to seize power. Soviets sprang up all over Germany and an Independent Socialist republic was set up in Bavaria.
- In January 1919 the **Spartacists** (communists) attempted a revolution in Berlin. The provisional government had to use the army and the *Freikorps* to regain control. The Spartacist leaders, Karl Liebknecht and Rosa Luxemburg, were murdered.
- In 1920, in the **Kapp putsch,** members of the *Freikorps* attempted to seize power. The putsch was badly organised and was soon brought to an end by a general strike in Berlin.

The currency crisis of 1923

- Germany faced severe economic problems at the end of the war with high unemployment and high inflation.
- The unexpectedly large reparations bill presented in 1921 made matters worse. To pay the reparations, the government printed paper money, resulting in further inflation.
- In 1923 it defaulted on its reparations payments. France responded by occupying the **Ruhr**. Passive resistance in the Ruhr brought Germany's greatest industrial area to a standstill. By November 1923, **hyper inflation** left the mark worthless.
- The crisis was defused by **Stresemann**, who became Chancellor in August 1923. He called off the campaign of passive resistance.
- In 1924 a new currency, the **Rentenmark**, was introduced, and the **Dawes Plan** scaled down the annual payments of reparations. The French then withdrew from the Ruhr.
- The currency crisis wiped out the savings of the middle classes and thus undermined their loyalty to the Weimar Republic.

The 'Golden Era' of Weimar, 1924–29

- In the period 1924–29, Germany enjoyed relative stability and prosperity.
- The economy recovered, industry entered on a period of expansion, unemployment decreased and living standards rose.
- This prosperity depended heavily on **foreign loans**.
- The **Dawes Plan** (1924) and the **Young Plan** (1929) reduced the burden of reparations.
- Stresemann restored Germany's position among the great powers. The Treaties of **Locarno** (1925), which guaranteed the 1919 frontiers with France and Belgium, took some of the bitterness out of Franco-German relations.
- Germany was admitted to the **League of Nations** in 1926 and was made a permanent member of the Council of the League.
- In 1928 it signed the **Kellogg-Briand Pact** to outlaw war as an instrument of policy.
- Politically there was relative **stability**. Coalitions were formed by the moderate parties. In the elections of 1924 and 1928, the extremists gained relatively small numbers of seats.
- But extremists of Right and Left were an unsettling influence, engaging in regular street battles.

Examiner's Tip

The stability of the Weimar republic was always fragile but its failure was not inevitable. Its history between 1925 and 1929 suggests that it might have succeeded but for the Great Depression.

The rise of Hitler

The rise of the Nazi Party

- Hitler joined the **German Workers' Party** in 1919. By 1921 he was its leader and the party had been re-named the National Socialist Party.
- Hitler quickly became known because of his **oratorical gifts**, which he used to attack Jews and Communists and to promise the restoration of national pride.
- The currency crisis of 1923 prompted Hitler to attempt to seize power by force – the **Beer Hall putsch**. The putsch was a rather pathetic failure, but Hitler's trial gained him national publicity. While in prison afterwards he wrote '**Mein Kampf'.**
- After the failure of the putsch, he decided to seek power through elections.
- Support for the Nazis declined after 1924. In the December 1924 elections, they won only 14 seats, and in 1928 only 12.
- Between 1924 and 1930, Hitler consolidated his hold over the party. Party organisation was strengthened: in each district, cells of party extremists were set up under the control of *gauleiters* appointed by Hitler. The SA gained recruits and conducted an increasingly violent campaign against Communist gangs.
- In 1930 the Nazis gained 107 seats in the Reichstag.

Hitler's beliefs and policies

- Hitler's **racial theories** were based on Social Darwinism. He believed that some races were inherently superior to others. In the highest category were the Aryan races, of which the Germans were the purest example.
- This was the basis for his **anti-Semitism**. He believed that the Jews were polluting other races (especially the Germans) by inter-marriage.
- He was a German **nationalist** who aimed to overthrow the Treaty of Versailles and unite all German peoples in a Greater Germany.
- He demanded **lebensraum** – living space for the Germans in Eastern Europe.
- He was strongly opposed to both communism and democracy.
- He placed great emphasis on propaganda and especially the value of the **'big lie'**. He made particularly effective use of the myth of **'the stab in the back'**.

Support for the Nazis

- Nazism drew its greatest support from the **middle classes**, many of whom feared that the weakness of Weimar governments might lead to a Communist revolution. The Great Depression intensified this fear and gave the Nazis increased middle-class support in the 1930s.
- **Industrialists** saw Hitler as a bulwark against 'red revolution' and began to finance the Nazis in the early 1930s.
- Peasant farmers were won over by pledges to reduce interest on agricultural debts.
- Some workers were attracted by the socialist element in the Nazi programme, but most remained loyal to the Socialist Party.
- Nazism appealed to the nationalist and anti-Semitic strands in German society.
- It made a strong impact on the young and particularly young males.
- Support for the Nazis was stronger among Protestants than Catholics.

Examiner's Tip

One of the strengths of National Socialism was that it appealed to German people from a variety of different backgrounds.

The downfall of the Weimar Republic

The crisis of Weimar, 1930–33

- The **Wall Street crash** affected Germany particularly badly because the economic recovery after 1924 depended on American loans. Unemployment shot up.
- In 1930 the coalition between the Social Democrats, the Centre Party and the People's Party collapsed.
- **President Hindenburg** appointed **Brüning**, leader of the Centre Party, as Chancellor. Unable to get a majority in the Reichstag, Brüning used the President's emergency powers to force through his proposed expenditure cuts.
- In the 1930 general election, the Nazis gained 107 seats and the Communists 77. It was impossible to construct a government with a majority in the Reichstag.
- In May 1932 Hindenburg dismissed Brüning and appointed **Papen**.
- In July the Nazis won 230 seats in the Reichstag elections, thus becoming the biggest party. Papen invited Hitler to join his cabinet, but he was not willing to accept any position other than that of Chancellor.
- In November Papen called another general election. The Nazis lost two million votes and 34 seats, while the Communists made substantial gains.
- Papen, still unable to gain a majority, resigned. **Schleicher**, who succeeded him, was also unable to form a government with a majority. Papen then did a deal with Hitler: Hitler would become Chancellor of a Nazi-Nationalist coalition government with Papen as Vice Chancellor. Hindenburg believed that Papen would be able to keep Hitler under control, and agreed.
- On 30 January 1933, Hitler was appointed **Chancellor**.

Why did the Weimar Republic fail?

- It was handicapped from the start because it was born of defeat in war and had to accepting humiliating terms at Versailles.
- Proportional representation led to unstable **coalitions**. In the end, it was impossible to form a government which commanded a majority in the Reichstag.
- The political leaders had no experience of democracy.
- The government had to rely on former servants of the Empire as civil servants, judges, teachers and, most importantly, army officers.
- Anti-democratic parties (Communists, Nationalists and National Socialists) had much support and were responsible for much violence.
- The mainstream political parties failed the Republic. The Socialists were more concerned with fighting their battle with the Communists than with saving democracy. The Centre Party under Brüning was happy to connive at the undermining of democracy by the use of the President's emergency powers.
- The Weimar Republic faced two severe economic crises. It survived the currency crisis of 1923 but not the Great Depression.
- Hindenburg's political outlook was anti-parliamentary. He was happy to allow democracy to wither through the use of his emergency powers.
- The manoeuvrings of the politicians in 1932 gave Hitler the chance to gain power by legal means. Papen was foolish to believe that he could control Hitler.

Examiner's Tip

The Weimar Republic had many handicaps but it was the Great Depression which allowed full rein to be given to the nationalistic and anti-democratic forces at work in Germany.

Nazi Germany: a totalitarian dictatorship

The consolidation of Hitler's power

- Hitler called another general election in March 1933.
- Nazi propaganda used the **Reichstag fire** to whip up anti-Communist feeling. Hitler made effective use of the radio to project his image. The SA made violent attacks on their opponents during the campaign.
- Even so, the Nazis only gained 44 per cent of the votes. With the support of the Nationalist Party, Hitler had a bare majority.
- On 23 March the **Enabling Law** was passed. This gave Hitler dictatorial powers.
- He then dissolved all other political parties.

The Night of the Long Knives

- Hitler still faced danger from the radical wing of the Nazi Party. **Röhm**, the leader of the SA, wanted Hitler to introduce a more socialist programme. He also wanted to absorb the army into the SA.
- On 30 June 1934 (the Night of the Long Knives), Röhm was murdered and some 400 others were removed by the SS.
- In August 1934, Hindenburg died. Hitler proclaimed himself **President, Chancellor and Führer**.

The National Socialist state

- Nazi Germany was a **totalitarian** state. Everything was subordinated to the good of the state.
- A highly developed **personality cult** depicted Hitler as the supremely wise leader, the focus of his people's aspirations.
- All organisations which might rival the Nazi party were either abolished or absorbed into the party. No other political parties were allowed. Trade unions were abolished and replaced by the **German Labour Front**. The state governments were put under the control of Nazi Reich Governors.
- All social organisations were subjected to *Gleichschaltung* – co-ordination, which in fact meant nazification.
- Nevertheless, much of the existing machinery of government survived alongside the Nazi organisations. The civil service continued to function efficiently.
- The overlapping functions of the state and the Party caused confusion and inefficiency. For example, the functions of ministers overlapped with those of Nazi Special Deputies.
- The first step towards security the two-thirds majority he needed to change the constitution was to arrest the communist deputies under an emergency law issued after the Reichstag fire.
- By a combination of false promises and intimidation he won the reluctant approval of the Catholic centre party.

Examiner's Tip

Hitler used the Weimar constitution to establish a totalitarian dictatorship. The Enabling Law was passed in an apparently constitutional manner, though only after the Communists had been excluded from the Reichstag.

Nazi Germany: the control of opinion

The Gestapo and the SS

- The **Gestapo** (secret police), set up in Prussia in 1933 by **Göring**, kept a close watch on possible opponents (communists, socialists, trade unionists) and people the Nazis disapproved of, such as Jews, gypsies and homosexuals.

- In 1936 **Himmler**, the head of the SS, became the police chief for the whole of Germany and the Gestapo came under his control.

- The **SS** was formed in 1925 as an élite paramilitary body within the Nazi Party. It had its own security service (the SD) under **Heydrich**, who was also, under Himmler, the head of the Gestapo. The combination of the SS, Gestapo and SD provided the Nazi state with the means to suppress any opposition by terror.

- The SS ran the **concentration camps**. Through the **Waffen SS** it had a leading role in the army. In the Second World War, it administered occupied territories and ran the extermination camps.

- The law courts were instruments of Nazi coercion. Judges were appointed for their loyalty to Nazi ideas.

Propaganda

- **Goebbels** was put in charge of a new Ministry of Propaganda in 1933. He established strict censorship of the press, books, films, and the arts.

Education and Youth

- In the schools, Nazi racial views were taught and textbooks were re-written. Teachers were required to join the Nazi Teachers' Association.

- Universities were placed under the control of government-appointed rectors.

- All youth movements were absorbed into the **Hitler Youth**. Boys joined at the age of 14 and were prepared for their future role in military service to the Nazi state.

- The **League of German Girls** prepared girls to serve the state as wives and mothers.

The churches

- Hitler saw the Catholic Church, which owed loyalty to the Pope in Rome, as a potential problem. In 1933, a **Concordat** with Rome ensured that the Catholic Church withdrew from politics in return for keeping some control over its schools. The Catholic Centre Party dissolved itself voluntarily.

- In 1937 Pope Pius XI issued an encyclical criticising the Nazi regime. Some Catholic priests continued to speak out against the Nazis and many were imprisoned.

- Many Protestants initially welcomed the Nazis in preference to what they regarded as the ungodly Weimar Republic.

- Hitler tried to bring the Protestant Churches under Nazi control by setting up the **Reich Church** under a Reich Bishop, Müller.

- This resulted in a split and the emergence of the Confessional Church, led by **Pastor Niemoller**. This was banned in 1937 and Niemoller and some hundreds of other pastors were sent to concentration camps.

Examiner's Tip

The churches did not become centres of opposition, but church members on the whole seem to have remained loyal to their faith and the churches continued to be a source of mute protest.

Nazi Germany: economic policies; anti-semitism

The economy

- Nazi economic policies had two main aims: to reduce unemployment and to revive Germany's military and industrial might.
- Economic activity was state-controlled. Wages, food prices, rents, investment and foreign exchange were all controlled. **Public works**, e.g. *autobahns*, were started, financed by the state.
- Trade unions were abolished and strikes made illegal.
- **Dr Schacht** created an elaborate system of exchange controls, which exploited the dependence of much of Eastern Europe upon Germany as a market for food exports. As a result, by 1935 exports exceeded imports.
- In 1936 a **Four-Year Plan** was introduced with the aim of making Germany ready for war within four years. The aim was to achieve self-sufficiency (autarky) by boosting domestic production and developing synthetic substitutes for oil and other imports. At the same time, a programme of large-scale **rearmament** was undertaken.

How successful were Nazi economic policies?

- Unemployment was reduced to two millions by 1935 and to virtually nil in 1939. The upturn in world trade from 1934 helped this. The public works schemes and rearmament provided a stimulus to economic activity.
- Conscription took half a million men out of the labour market.
- Some of the reduction in unemployment was artificial. The civil service and the party organisation were over-staffed.
- The removal of political opponents and 'undesirables' to concentration camps reduced unemployment because they were not counted. Neither were Jews.
- Despite massive investment, synthetic substitutes for oil and rubber only produced a small proportion of Germany's needs.
- Agriculture failed to meet its targets and Germany continued to depend on food imports.
- The massive cost of rearmament produced a risk of runaway inflation. Some historians claim that by 1939, war was the only answer to Germany's economic problems.

The Jews

- The Jews were singled out for special persecution as the scapegoats for all Germany's ills. They were blamed especially for the 'stab in the back'.
- In 1933 there was a **boycott** of Jewish shops and businesses. Jews were dismissed from the civil service and excluded from universities and the professions.
- In 1935 the **Nuremberg Laws** deprived Jews of German citizenship and forbade them to marry 'Aryans'.
- In 1938 attacks on synagogues and Jewish houses and businesses took place all over Germany (**Kristallnacht** – the Night of Broken Glass).
- The **'final solution'** began in 1941 with mass deportations of Jews to concentration camps. Between 1942 and 1945 some three to four million Jews died in the gas chambers.

Examiner's Tip

Historians debate whether Hitler intended to exterminate the Jews from the start or decided upon it as a result of the war in the east, which closed off the possibility of mass deportation. Few historians doubt his personal responsibility.

The German army and the German people

The army

- Until 1938, the army was the most powerful institution which was not fully under Hitler's control. But in August 1934, when Hitler took the title of *Führer*, all members of the army were required to take an oath of personal allegiance to him. Military ideas of personal honour made it difficult for army officers to oppose Hitler after this.

- Between 1934 and 1938 the army was gradually brought under Nazi control.

- The general staff became increasingly worried by the trend of foreign policy.

- In November 1937, as recorded in the **Hossbach memorandum**, Hitler announced to his chief military advisers his plans for the expansion of Germany. Horrified by the risk of war with Britain and France, the generals protested.

- Hitler's response was to reorganise the command structure of the army. The War Minister, **Blomberg**, and the Commander-in-Chief of the Army, **Fritsch**, were both dismissed in 1938 on charges of personal misconduct. Hitler put the army under his direct command through the OKW.

- In 1938 General **Beck** tried to persuade the General Staff to remove Hitler, but he received no support and resigned.

- In 1944 **Stauffenberg** placed a bomb in Hitler's conference room in East Prussia but Hitler survived.

The response of the German people to Nazism

- Industrialists saw Hitler as a bulwark against communism. They welcomed the abolition of trade unions. Big business profited from rearmament and from the war effort. In return it provided much of the money to finance the Nazi party.

- The middle classes were impressed by Hitler's success in restoring prosperity, in warding off the threat of communist revolution and in rebuilding national pride.

- The working classes were pleased by the drop in unemployment, by rent controls and by the benefits offered by the Strength through Joy organisation, such as subsidised holidays.

- Farmers were won over by fixed prices for their products and by a law which made farms hereditary estates.

- The status of women suffered. The Nazis taught that their function was to serve the state by producing children. Women were eased out of professional positions and the civil service. In the later 1930s, however, labour shortages created a demand for women workers in agriculture and industry.

Examiner's Tip

There can be little doubt that Hitler was popular in the 1930s. The Nazis succeeded in reducing unemployment, restoring prosperity, establishing strong and stable government and reviving Germany's power in Europe.

Progress check

1 Why did many Germans regard the November Revolution as a 'stab in the back'?

2 Under the Weimar constitution, how was the Reichstag elected and what were its powers?

3 What effect did proportional representation have on the government of Germany?

4 Why did many Germans regard the Treaty of Versailles as a *diktat*?

5 How did the Weimar government overcome (a) the Spartacist Rising and (b) the Kapp Putsch?

6 Why did the French occupy the Ruhr in 1923?

7 What did Germany gain from the Dawes Plan?

8 How did the currency crisis of 1923 affect the German middle classes?

9 How did the Treaty of Locarno improve relations between Germany and France?

10 What did Hitler mean when he talked of the 'November criminals'?

11 What was the importance of Hitler's demand for 'lebensraum'?

12 Why did Hitler gain much support from the middle classes?

13 Why did Brüning rely on the President's emergency powers from 1930?

14 Name, in order, the successive Chancellors in 1932–33.

15 Compare the results for the Nazis of the two general elections of 1932.

16 What was Hindenburg's attitude towards the Weimar system of government and why was it important?

17 How did the Reichstag fire help Hitler to consolidate his power?

18 How did Hitler secure the two-thirds majority he needed to pass the Enabling Law?

19 What political purposes did the Night of the Long Knives serve for Hitler?

20 What was *gleichschaltung*?

21 What positions did Himmler hold in the Nazi government?

22 Distinguish between the SA and the SS.

23 What message did the League of German Girls try to convey to its members?

24 What was agreed in the Concordat between Germany and the Pope in 1933?

25 Why was the fact that Hitler took the title of *Führer* important for his relations with the army?

26 What was the Hossbach Memorandum?

27 Why were Generals Fritsch and Blomberg dismissed in 1938?

28 What was the Confessional Church?

29 What was autarky and how did the Nazis try to achieve it?

30 What was *Kristallnacht*?

Answers on page 93–94

GERMANY, 1918–45

80 AS History Revision Notes

Soviet Russia, 1917–53

Lenin, 1917–24

The consolidation of Bolshevik power

Lenin took several crucial decisions in the early days of Bolshevik rule in order to fulfil the promises of 'land, peace and bread' and 'all power to the soviets'.

- Land was **confiscated** from the crown, the Church and the landowners and redistributed to the peasants.

- The Constituent Assembly, which met in January 1918, was immediately dissolved by Red Guards because the Bolsheviks were in a minority. The All-Russian Congress of Soviets then considered Lenin's proposals for the constitution.

- Peace was made with Germany and Austria at **Brest-Litovsk** (March 1918). Despite the severe terms, Lenin insisted that there was no alternative to accepting it.

- **War Communism** was instituted. Industry and the banks were nationalised. Private trade was forbidden. Peasants were made to sell all surplus grain to the state at fixed prices. Lenin later claimed that War Communism was an emergency measure, but it is more likely that it was an attempt to introduce doctrinaire communist ideas.

- In December 1917 Lenin set up the **Cheka** (secret police) which instituted the 'Red Terror'. By February 1922, when the Cheka was replaced by the OGPU, Lenin was satisfied that all opposition had been suppressed.

The Soviet constitution

- In July 1918 the new Soviet constitution was introduced. Russia became the Russian Soviet Federated Socialist Republic.

- Supreme power nominally lay with the **All-Russian Congress of Soviets**, but this only met for about one week each year. The Congress elected an Executive Committee, which in turn elected the ten members of the Council of People's Commissars (ministers).

- The Commissars were members of the **Politburo** of the Communist Party, which was where real power lay. No other political parties were allowed.

- In 1922 the **Union of Soviet Socialist Republics** was set up. This was a federation of republics, of which Russia was the most important.

The Civil War

- The Bolshevik seizure of power led to civil war between 1918 and 1920. The **Whites** (counter-revolutionaries) attacked from the south, the east and the Baltic.

- **Foreign powers** intervened because they feared that the Russian Revolution would lead to revolutions elsewhere. Britain and France were also angry at Russia's desertion of the Allied cause in the war.

- Foreign forces intervened in Archangel and Murmansk in the north, in the Crimea and the Caucasus in the south, and in Siberia.

- By 1920 the Bolsheviks had overcome most of the White forces.

- Then Russia was attacked by **Poland**, which, with French aid, succeeded in taking over a substantial part of White Russia and the Ukraine (Treaty of Riga, 1921).

(Continued next page)

Lenin, 1917–24

Why did the Communists (Reds) win the Civil War?

- The **Red Army** was united under a single command, that of **Trotsky**, who created an efficient fighting machine by sheer personal dynamism. By the end of the Civil War, the Red Army numbered over five million men.
- The Communists controlled the main cities and the railways. They therefore had the advantage of internal communications.
- The peasants feared that the Whites would return the land to the landlords.
- Foreign intervention enabled the Communists to pose as Russian patriots.
- The Whites were not united in their aims. Some were Tsarists, others republicans.
- The Whites also lacked co-ordination. This was partly a matter of geography – transport and communication between the White forces were difficult.
- The foreign supporters of the Whites were half-hearted.

The New Economic Policy, 1921

- By 1921 the economy was on the verge of collapse. Under War Communism, the government took all surplus agricultural produce. The peasants therefore stopped producing more than they needed for themselves. The result was famine, aggravated by droughts in 1920–21.
- There were widespread disturbances. The naval **mutiny at Kronstadt** in 1921 convinced Lenin that a change was needed.
- The **New Economic Policy** allowed the peasants to sell their surplus produce on payment of a tax of a percentage of the crop. It also restored private trading through *Nepmen*. All major industrial installations, however, remained under state control, as did banking, transport and foreign trade.

Assessment of Lenin

- He played a crucial role in 1917 in the overthrow of the Provisional government.
- His decisions about the land and the peace with Germany enabled the Bolsheviks to hold on to power.
- With the help of Trotsky and the Red Army, he held the new Communist state together through the Civil War.
- His decision to replace War Communism by the New Economic Policy was realistic, even though it involved compromising the basic principles of Marxism.
- He made a start on social reform with decrees providing free education and a national insurance scheme.
- He achieved some foreign recognition for Soviet Russia, including the resumption of full diplomatic relations with Germany by the **Treaty of Rapallo** (1922).
- He was completely ruthless: millions of Russians died in the civil war and the great famine of 1920–21, and thousands more were victims of the secret police.
- The new Russian state which he created was a totalitarian police state. It had a vast bureaucracy, meshed with the Communist Party.
- His failure to make arrangements for choosing his successor allowed Stalin to take over eventually.

Examiner's Tip

It can be argued that Stalinism was the direct consequence of the totalitarian system created by Lenin. But it is also possible that he would have modified it if he had lived.

Stalin's dictatorship, 1924–41

Rise to power

- Stalin became Commissar for Nationalities in 1917 and General Secretary of the Communist Party in 1922. This position enabled him to build up a power base because the Secretariat controlled membership of the Party at local level.

- After Lenin's death, **Kamenev** and **Zinoviev** joined Stalin in the Triumvirate. This isolated **Trotsky**, who was forced to resign as Commissar for War in 1925.

- In 1926–27 Stalin allied himself to **Bukharin**, who advocated continuing with the New Economic Policy, while Kamenev and Zinoviev joined forces with Trotsky to demand that it should be abandoned.

- At the Party Congress in 1927, Stalin triumphed. Trotsky, Kamenev and Zinoviev were removed from the Politburo. In 1929, Trotsky was sent into exile.

- In 1929 Stalin broke with Bukharin and his 'rightist' colleagues. They too were removed from the Politburo. Stalin was left as undisputed dictator.

Why did Stalin win the battle for the succession to Lenin?

- He displayed great political skill in out-manoeuvring his rivals.

- As General Secretary he had built up solid support in the Party Congress.

- He advocated **'Socialism in one country'**, which had more appeal than **'permanent revolution'** to Russians, who simply wanted peace and prosperity after the First World War and the Civil War.

- Trotsky was mistrusted, as being too clever, too western in his ways of thought and too inclined to think he was right and the Party wrong.

Economic policy: the Five-Year Plans

- The first Five-Year Plan (1928–32) concentrated on heavy industry. The second (1933–37) allowed for limited production of consumer goods but the third (1938–42) returned to the emphasis on heavy industry (and also armaments).

- Targets were set for all major industries and success was achieved by putting great pressure on the workforce. Russia was transformed into **a major industrial power**.

- Discipline in the factories was strict. Wages were low and housing in the new industrial towns was poor. Government propaganda stressed that the sacrifices were in a patriotic cause.

- There were also incentives: pay differentials and medals for outstanding workers (**Stakhanovites**). Also, by the mid-1930s, workers began to see some benefits in education, health care and holidays with pay.

- Since foreign loans were not available to Communist Russia, capital had to be raised by cutting labour costs to the minimum and ploughing back all surpluses.

- To earn foreign exchange to pay for imports of machinery, Russia depended on grain exports. The success of the Five-Year Plans therefore depended on agriculture.

The collectivisation of agriculture

- Russian agriculture was inefficient because most of the peasant farms were too small to use modern agricultural machinery.

- The rise of a class of richer peasants (**kulaks**), who owned their own land and had profited from the New Economic Policy, was contrary to Communist ideology.

(Continued next page)

Stalin's dictatorship, 1924–41

- Stalin therefore decided on **collectivisation**. The *kulaks* resisted by burning their crops and slaughtering their cattle. Between 1929 and 1932 there was virtual civil war in the countryside, resulting in **famine** in 1932–33.
- By 1939, 97 per cent of all land had been collectivised. There were record grain harvests in the late 1930s, but agriculture was still relatively inefficient.
- At least ten million *kulaks* were killed, died in the famine or were deported to Siberia.

The purges

- The purges were sparked off by the murder of the Communist Party boss in Leningrad, **Kirov**.
- **Zinoviev and Kamenev** were arrested and imprisoned in 1935, and executed in 1936 after a show trial. Another show trial in 1938 removed **Bukharin and Yagoda**, the head of the NKVD (secret police).
- All the possible rivals to Stalin were liquidated: all the living members of Lenin's politburo except Stalin himself and Trotsky (in exile); the Chief of the General Staff and about two thirds of the senior officers in the army. About 300 000 lesser people were shot and seven million were sent to labour camps in Arctic Russia and Siberia (the *gulags*).
- Stalin was left in total control of a terrorised population, but Russia was deprived of many of its best brains.

Stalin's Russia

- Nominally the USSR was a democracy. The **Constitution of 1936** provided for all citizens over 18 to elect the Supreme Soviet. But there was only one party to vote for. Real power lay with the Communist Party and ultimately its Secretary, Stalin.
- The Soviet Union was a police state. The secret police, the **OGPU**, enforced collectivisation. In 1934 it was merged with the **NKVD**, which became notorious as the instrument by which Stalin carried out the purges.
- There was strict censorship of the press. There was no freedom of speech and little freedom of movement.
- The USSR was a **totalitarian** state. All forms of opposition or disagreement were suppressed. The national minorities were suppressed. Jews were persecuted. The Orthodox Church was attacked: priests were persecuted and churches closed.

Education and culture

- Education was closely supervised to ensure that Marxist doctrines of the class struggle and the dictatorship of the proletariat were inculcated. Teachers were required to promote Stalinist ideology.
- Illiteracy was almost eradicated and it became possible for working-class children to enter higher education.
- Cultural life was state-controlled. Writers, artists and musicians were required to produce works of **'socialist realism'**.
- Stalin became the object of an extraordinary **personality cult**. Propaganda portrayed him as the great leader who cared for his people and on whom everything depended. Everywhere there were statues or portraits of him.

Examiner's Tip

In spite of his brutal methods, Stalin enjoyed overwhelming support. He achieved remarkable growth in Russia's industrial power.

The Second World War

Stalin's foreign policy in the 1920s and 1930s

- In the 1920s the USSR was **isolated** from international diplomacy.
- In 1934 the USSR joined the **League of Nations**.
- At first, Stalin was not alarmed by the rise of Hitler. When he realised his error, he tried to improve relations with the west, but in the end he concluded that the western powers would not help Russia against Germany.
- He therefore decided to seek an agreement with Germany. The **German-Soviet Pact** (1939) enabled him to regain the territory lost to Poland in 1921.
- Stalin went on to attack **Finland**. Despite unexpectedly stiff resistance by the Finns, Russia gained territory in Karelia. It also annexed the Baltic states.
- Relations with Germany deteriorated but Stalin was convinced that Hitler would not attack Russia while still at war in the west. He was completely taken by surprise when Hitler launched **Operation Barbarossa** in June 1941.

The Great Patriotic War

- In 1941–42 the Germans advanced deep into Russia. By the end of 1941, they had captured Kiev, Odessa and the Crimea, had almost reached Moscow and were besieging Leningrad. Only the Russian winter halted their advance.
- In 1942 the main German offensive was in the south. In September they attacked **Stalingrad**, but in February 1943 the combination of the Russian winter and over-extended supply lines forced them to surrender. This was the turning point of the war.
- In 1943 the Russian armies began to push the Germans back. In July they won the tank battle at **Kursk**. In November Kiev was liberated and early in 1944, Leningrad.
- In the second half of 1944, the Red Army advanced into Eastern Europe, occupying Rumania, Bulgaria and Poland. In March 1945, Russian troops entered eastern Germany, reaching **Berlin** in April.

Why was the USSR victorious?

- Hitler's refusal to allow a retreat from Stalingrad was a serious mistake.
- The rapid advance of the German armies left them with over-extended lines of communication.
- By the brutal treatment of the Russians in German-occupied territory, Hitler threw away the chance to turn them against Stalin's dictatorship.
- Stalin himself provided a **focus of leadership**, which he used to great effect to mobilise Russian patriotism.
- He set up the **State Defence Committee** in 1941 to organise and co-ordinate the war effort. He reorganised the army and promoted able officers.
- Russia's industrial strength, together with massive aid from the USA and Britain, enabled it to equip its vast army.
- The State Defence Committee organised a massive transfer of industrial plant from the war zone to Siberia and Central Asia. In the latter years of the war, the USSR was producing more military equipment than Germany and of better quality.

Examiner's Tip

The cost of the war to Russia was enormous. Overall, the USSR lost 23 million dead, including three millions who died as prisoners of war in German hands. Five million people were homeless.

The Cold War

Relations between the USSR and the West

- The war temporarily transformed Russia's relations with the West. In 1942 the **Grand Alliance** of the USA, Britain and the USSR was formed.

- The alliance with the western powers was rather uneasy. Stalin accused the USA and Britain of failing to take the pressure off Russia in 1943 by postponing the invasion of France.

- Stalin suspected that the Western powers would ultimately try to overthrow Communism in Russia. He therefore wanted a Communist-controlled Eastern Europe as a buffer against the perceived threat from the west.

- In 1944–45 Britain and the USA became increasingly suspicious of Russian intentions in Eastern Europe. At the **Yalta** Conference in 1945, they insisted that nations conquered by the Germans should decide their future through free and democratic elections.

- By 1946, however, Stalin had established Communist governments in Poland, Rumania, Bulgaria and Hungary. Yugoslavia and Albania also had Communist governments established by partisans. A Communist coup in Czechoslovakia in 1948 completed Soviet **control of Eastern Europe**.

- To the western powers, this looked like a Communist threat to the whole of Europe. Because of this, the USA began to strengthen its ties with Western Europe.

- When the western powers began to rebuild Western Germany, Stalin tightened his control over the Eastern European satellite states. In 1949, he set up **Comecon** to co-ordinate their economies and direct their trade towards Russia.

- By the early 1950s there were five and a half million Soviet troops in Eastern Europe.

- In 1948 Stalin cut off the western sectors of **Berlin** from the west, hoping to force the western powers to abandon it. Instead, they overcame the blockade by the Air Lift, and then went on to set up the **Federal Republic** in Western Germany.

- In 1949 the western powers created **NATO** to defend themselves against the threat they perceived from Russia to Western Europe.

- In 1950–53 the Cold War spread to the Far East in the **Korean War**.

Stalin's last years, 1945–53

- The major task facing Russia in 1945 was **reconstruction**. The fourth and fifth Five-Year Plans rebuilt Russian industry. By 1950 the USSR was the world's second biggest industrial power.

- The nuclear industry was developed. By 1949 the USSR had an **atomic bomb**.

- The standard of living was low, partly because of the emphasis on capital goods in the Five-Year Plans, but also because of the high level of military expenditure.

- The repression of the 1930s was renewed.

- Stalin was obsessed by fears of a hostile world seeking to destroy the USSR, and cut Russia off from the outside world. He became obsessed by real and imaginary threats to himself and was planning new purges when he died in 1953.

Examiner's Tip

When Stalin died, the USSR was ruled by a savagely repressive dictatorship, and its people were isolated from the rest of the world. But it was also one of the two superpowers.

Progress check

1 What were the main features of War Communism?

2 What was the *Cheka*?

3 What was the *Politburo* and who were its members?

4 What were the main reasons for foreign intervention in the Civil War?

5 What did Russia lose by the Treaty of Riga?

6 What part did Trotsky play in the Communist victory in the Civil War?

7 Why did peasants support the Communists in the Civil War?

8 What was Lenin's response to the mutiny at Kronstadt?

9 What were *Nepmen*?

10 Who were the members of the Triumvirate?

11 Which of the rivals for power after the death of Lenin stood for 'permanent revolution' and what did he mean by it?

12 What sort of industries did Stalin wish to build up by the Five-Year Plans?

13 What were Stakhanovites?

14 Why did Stalin embark on a policy of collectivisation of agriculture?

15 Who were the most important victims of the purges?

16 What was the NKVD and what part did it play in the purges?

17 What was Stalin's policy towards the Orthodox Church?

18 What was 'socialist realism'?

19 What territories did Stalin conquer or annex in 1939–40?

20 What was Comecon?

21 Why was Stalin suspicious of the aims of Britain and the USA at the end of the Second World War?

22 What did he hope to achieve by the Berlin blockade of 1948?

Answers on page 94

Progress check answers

The age of reform, 1815–46

1 The Corn Laws; indirect taxes following the abolition of income tax.
2 It allowed suspects to be imprisoned without trial.
3 Reduction of import duties; relaxation of Navigation Acts; reciprocity agreements; preferential duties for the colonies.
4 Because they feared civil war in Ireland.
5 Over-representation of the south and under-representation of the north and Scotland; new industrial towns not represented.
6 £10 householders in the boroughs; 40 shilling freeholders, £10 copyholders and £50 leaseholders in the counties.
7 Demands for further reform in the future.
8 Not much – MPs were still mainly from the landed class.
9 It was the first effective Act – four inspectors were appointed.
10 £20 000; the National Society and the British and Foreign Society.
11 Wages of agricultural labourers were supplemented in accordance with the size of their families and the price of bread.
12 Conditions in workhouses were to be less attractive than those for the poorest labourers outside them.
13 Cobden and Bright.
14 It would promote peace through trade.
15 The most important were Lovett, Attwood and O'Connor.
16 Support for it rose and fell in response to economic conditions.
17 To accept the Reform Act and to reform proved abuses.
18 Reduction of duties (free trade) and reintroduction of income tax.
19 Because the Conservative Party was the party of the Church of England and Maynooth College was a training college for Catholic priests.
20 Because the Conservative Party was the party of the landowners; they argued it would ruin agriculture.

England, 1846–86

1 It split between Peelites and Protectionists.
2 It brought the Whigs and Peelites together to form the Liberal Party.
3 Because he stood up for British interests in his foreign policy.
4 Since the electorate in the larger boroughs was too big to bribe, efficient local organisation became essential.
5 Because Church schools were to receive increased government grants.
6 It made picketing (even peaceful picketing) illegal; Gladstone lost the support of trade union members.
7 They removed privileges in entry to the civil service, commissions in the army, and teaching posts in the universities.
8 (a) Male householders and £10 lodgers in the boroughs, and £12 leaseholders in the counties. (b) Male householders in the counties.
9 (a) Tenants were to be compensated for improvements unless evicted for non-payment of rent. (b) The three Fs.
10 Rent strikes and boycotts, obstruction of business in parliament.
11 Gladstone would introduce an Act to wipe out arrears of rent and Parnell would call off the rent strike.
12 Convinced English opinion that the Irish were not fit to govern themselves.
13 Split it: Chamberlain and Hartington led a substantial minority of Liberal Unionists who opposed Home Rule.
14 Because of his involvement in the O'Shea divorce.
15 (a) The Commons. (b) The Lords.
16 Protestants in Ulster believed Home Rule would mean Rome rule.
17 Disraeli introduced more social reforms than Gladstone, who was more interested in institutional reform.
18 It made peaceful picketing legal.
19 He persuaded Russia to accept modification of the settlement which it had imposed on Turkey; Britain gained Cyprus.
20 The Afghan and Zulu Wars made imperialism seem dangerous.

Foreign affairs, 1815–1902

1 Britain, Austria, Prussia and Russia.
2 (a) Asserted the right of the great powers to intervene in countries where there were revolutions. (b) Opposed intervention.
3 To admit France to the Congress System.
4 Canning was more favourable to liberal movements and better at gaining public support for his policies.
5 Because they were important for British trade.
6 France and Russia.
7 Guaranteed the neutrality of Belgium.
8 Because it gave Russia control over the Dardanelles and thus access to the Mediterranean.
9 The Dardanelles was closed to warships of all nations in time of peace.
10 Because he wished to preserve Austria as a bulwark against Russia.
11 It was neutralised – Russia was not allowed to have a navy there.
12 Gladstone wanted the Turks to be removed from the Balkans because of their brutality; Disraeli wanted to preserve Turkey as a bulwark against Russia.
13 He feared that 'big' Bulgaria would be under Russian control.
14 Markets for British manufactures, sources of raw materials, outlets for investment.
15 He wanted it to develop into a single economic and political unit.
16 Any power which occupied African land became its possessor; this opened the way for the scramble for Africa.
17 British and French forces came face to face but the French eventually withdrew.
18 They were denied political rights and heavily taxed.
19 It poisoned them.
20 The colonies he built up surrounded the Boer republics. (Also the Jameson Raid.)

The Edwardian age

1 Because it provided support from the rates for church schools.
2 Britain would have a free hand in Egypt and France in Morocco.
3 It supported France against Germany.
4 It split it and led to its defeat in the 1906 election.
5 New Liberalism was collectivist and keen on social reform; Gladstonian Liberalism was individualist and not very interested in social reform.
6 Free school meals and medical treatment for needy children, compulsory medical inspections, juvenile courts and borstals.
7 To fix minimum wages in the 'sweated' industries, where the workers were not organised into trade unions and were therefore very poorly paid.
8 Those over 70 with an income below £21 p.a.
9 Contributions from workers, employers and the state.
10 Taxes on the wealthy, especially the tax on land values.
11 Not allowed to reject money bills, two-year delaying power for other bills.
12 It made it possible to overcome the opposition of the Lords to Home Rule.
13 It showed the government could not rely on the army to enforce Home Rule.
14 Britain relied on the navy for defence, whereas Germany was primarily a land power.
15 Britain would concentrate its naval strength in the North Sea and France in the Mediterranean.
16 The despatch of the German gunboat 'Panther' to Agadir.
17 Formed a war cabinet (5 members) and set up Cabinet Secretariat to co-ordinate the departments.
18 All men over 21 and women over 30.
19 Allowed married women to own property – previously their property was legally their husband's.
20 Suffragists relied on persuasion, suffragettes adopted militant tactics.
21 Suffragettes who went on hunger strike in prison could be released and then re-arrested when they were restored to health.
22 Subscriptions were high; provided unemployment and sickness benefits; tried to avoid strikes.
23 The right to protect their funds in court.
24 It proved that unskilled workers could organise a successful strike.

25 The 'New' unions were for unskilled workers, had low subscriptions and were more militant than the new model unions.
26 Keir Hardie; to secure the election of MPs who would represent the interests of the working classes.
27 It made it impossible to organise strikes because they would bankrupt the union.

28 It enabled Labour to gain 29 MPs in 1906.
29 To impose a political levy, subject to contracting out.
30 It emphasised the distinction between the Labour and Liberal parties and committed Labour to nationalisation (Clause 4).

The inter-war years

1 Supporters of the coalition were identified by a letter from party leaders (the 'coupon').
2 Expenditure cuts, affecting mainly education, housing and the armed forces.
3 The Triple Alliance (miners, railwaymen and transport workers) collapsed.
4 The Irish Free State was set up but the six counties of Northern Ireland remained part of the United Kingdom.
5 To investigate the problems of the coal industry (and to try to avert a strike).
6 Emergency plans to safeguard food supplies and transport and to maintain order.
7 General or sympathetic strikes were made illegal and the political levy was made subject to contracting in.
8 The Wheatley Housing Act and increases in old age pensions and unemployment benefits.
9 It scared voters into believing that there was a danger of a communist revolution and thus benefited the Conservatives.

10 Because the cabinet could not agree about expenditure cuts, especially in unemployment benefit.
11 Because he accepted office as Prime Minister of a National Government.
12 It helped it by making exports cheaper.
13 Imperial preference.
14 Public works, which would create jobs and stimulate economic activity.
15 Because the older export industries, such as coal, textiles and shipbuilding, were concentrated there.
16 To help the older industrial areas.
17 He saw it as a sign of weakness.
18 It gained experience of government.
19 It enabled Britain to buy American goods on credit.
20 Churchill was replaced by Attlee, because Labour won the 1945 election.

Post-war Britain, 1945–64

1 It persuaded voters that Labour would build a better society for post-war Britain.
2 Want, disease, ignorance, squalor and idleness.
3 By National Insurance contributions and taxation.
4 It provided secondary education for all children and raised the school leaving age to 15.
5 Over a million houses were built but because of demographic changes there was still a shortage.
6 Its delaying power was reduced to one year.
7 The Bank of England, air transport, Cable and Wireless, coal, rail, docks, canals, road haulage, electricity, gas and iron and steel.
8 That sterling should be made convertible – it led to a balance of payments crisis.
9 A sharp rise in the cost of imported raw materials.
10 Because of the introduction of health service charges to pay for the Korean War.

11 Rationing, austerity, controls, housing shortage.
12 Because of the religious division between Hindus and Muslims.
13 The Truman Doctrine.
14 US aid to rebuild the European economies.
15 50 per cent increase in house building.
16 He believed in social reform.
17 Economic policy of successive phases of controls to deal with balance of payments deficits and relaxations when balance of payments moved into surplus.
18 Rising standard of living – wages rose faster than prices – people able to afford more consumer goods.
19 It was vetoed by France.
20 Modernisation, planned economy, encouragement of technological change.

France, 1814–75

1 Constitutional monarchy, freedom of speech and the press, religious toleration and equality before the law.
2 Return of land and power to émigré nobles and to the Church.
3 Purge of Bonapartists.
4 Led to reduction of rights granted in the Charter, especially freedom of the press.
5 It showed that Charles X intended to restore the Church to its pre-1789 position.
6 Dissolved Chamber of Deputies and reduced the electorate; virtually destroyed the Charter.
7 Because he was a typical bourgeois; also his father had supported the Revolution.
8 The 'right to work' – state should provide 'National Workshops'.
9 Subservience to Britain; 'boring'.
10 He was anti-liberal. His government was corrupt. Above all, refused to consider widening the franchise.
11 Rising of the Paris working classes – aroused fear among Frenchmen outside Paris, especially the middle classes, of 'red revolution'.
12 Support of Catholic opinion.
13 Appointed ministers, controlled foreign policy and armed services, initiated legislation.
14 Assembly was given power to propose laws and vote on the budget; ministry formed representing the majority in the Assembly.
15 Rebuilding of Paris – creation of boulevards and squares.
16 (a) Catholics feared for the papacy; (b) liberals disapproved of Truce of Villafranca because Napoleon abandoned support for Italians.
17 It led to the creation of a major power in western Germany.
18 It would mean France faced Hohenzollern kings to the east and the south-west; also opposing it would enable Napoleon to regain lost prestige.
19 Loss of Alsace-Lorraine, army of occupation, indemnity.
20 Division between supporters of Bourbon and Orleans claimants.

Russia, 1825–1917

1 A national assembly for Russia.
2 The secret police under Nicholas I.
3 Placed under military rule; Polish nationalism suppressed.
4 Because the *mir* was collectively responsible for redemption payments.
5 District councils, elected on a system which favoured the nobility and gentry.
6 Trial by jury and in public, salaries for judges.
7 A revolutionary movement which aimed to educate the peasants to demand reforms.
8 (a) Secret police; (b) armed attack on Jews.
9 It split between Bolsheviks, who wanted an élite party of revolutionaries and Mensheviks, who wanted a mass party of the working class.
10 Defeat in the Russo-Japanese War.
11 Troops opened fire on a procession of peaceful unarmed demonstrators carrying a petition to the Tsar.
12 A Duma elected on a fairly wide franchise and with legislative powers.
13 It demanded sweeping reforms, including a democratic electoral system.
14 The Octobrists – moderate liberals.
15 He blamed Witte for forcing him to issue the October Manifesto.
16 To create a class of prosperous peasants and thus make agriculture more efficient; he also hoped this class would support the Tsardom.
17 Tannenberg and the Masurian Lakes.
18 Lenin set out the aim of 'all power to the soviets', which meant overthrowing the Provisional Government.
19 Because of rumours that land was to be redistributed.
20 (a) Prime Minister of the Provisional Government from February to July 1917; (b) general who attempted a right-wing coup in September 1917.

PROGRESS CHECK ANSWERS

The unification of Italy

1 Piedmont-Sardinia.
2 A secret society of Italian republican revolutionaries.
3 Making Italy united, independent and free; Mazzini.
4 To unite northern Italy into a kingdom under his rule.
5 Because he had the reputation of being a liberal. The papacy was in any case the natural focus of leadership for many Italians.
6 A confederation of Italian states under the Pope.
7 Sicily and Naples.
8 Napoleon III sent French troops.
9 Piedmont was defeated at the battles of Custozza and Novara.
10 That foreign assistance was needed to defeat the Austrians.
11 So that Piedmont could win the sympathy of Britain and France and could raise Italy's grievances at the peace conference.
12 An agreement between France and Piedmont to expel the Austrians from Lombardy and Venetia.
13 Napoleon III's agreement with Austria to withdraw from the war, leaving Venetia in Austrian hands.
14 Parma, Modena, Tuscany and the Romagna.
15 He feared Garibaldi would go on to attack Rome, which could lead to war with France.
16 He sent troops into the Papal States to link up with Garibaldi; but they avoided attacking Rome.
17 As a result of the Seven Weeks' War between Austria and Prussia in 1866, in which Italy allied with Prussia.
18 Because French troops were stationed there.
19 French troops were withdrawn because of the Franco-Prussian War.
20 A constitutional monarchy.

The unification of Germany

1 Because it would mean including in Germany many Slav peoples from the Austrian Empire.
2 The Confederation was revived.
3 A customs union which established free trade throughout most of Germany except Austria.
4 Because of a crisis with the Prussian Parliament over financing an increase in the size of the army.
5 The North German Confederation excluded Austria and the South German states (Bavaria, Baden and Württemberg).
6 By altering it he was able to provoke a war with France, which he thought was bound to come sooner or later.
7 Alsace and Lorraine became part of Germany; France was to pay an indemnity and accept an army of occupation.
8 By revealing that Napoleon III had had an eye on Belgium in 1866 as 'compensation' for Prussia's gains in the Seven Weeks' War.
9 They gave Prussia a highly efficient army, which enabled it to defeat Austria and France.
10 The Kaiser; it meant that the Reichstag had no power over the government.
11 A veto over legislation and control over the federal budget.
12 The size of the army and the introduction of tariffs.
13 Sickness and accident insurance and old age pensions, introduced by Bismarck in 1883–89.
14 Good relations: Austria and Russia. Isolation: France.
15 War between Russia and Austria.
16 Triple Alliance: Germany, Austria, Italy. Dreikaiserbund: Germany, Austria, Russia.
17 (a) Support for Weltpolitik; (b) protection for agriculture.
18 Prussian gentry; they controlled the government of Prussia and therefore the Bundesrat, which consisted of representatives of the states.
19 The anti-Socialist laws, colonial policy and relations with Russia.
20 Caprivi, Hohenlohe, Bülow and Bethmann-Hollweg.
21 World policy – demand that Germany should have 'a place in the sun'.
22 He hoped to undermine the Anglo-French entente but in fact strengthened it.
23 To make it a world power and able to compete with Britain.
24 Because it was denied Albania, which it wanted for access to the sea.
25 It promised to support Austria without conditions.

Italy, 1919–45

1   South Tyrol, Trentino, Trieste and part of Istria.
2   Italy was denied the rest of Istria and Fiume (which caused most anger).
3   The system of bribery and corruption by which Italian parliaments were managed between 1860 and 1914.
4   Fighting groups formed by Mussolini in Milan in 1919.
5   Law that the party which gained most votes in a general election would have two-thirds of the seats in the Chamber of Deputies.
6   He had publicly blamed Mussolini for the violence during the 1924 election campaign. His murder led to demands for Mussolini's dismissal, but the king refused.
7   Opposition members left parliament in protest against the King's refusal to dismiss Mussolini after the murder of Matteotti. It helped Mussolini because it left him in control of parliament.
8   It saw him as a bulwark against the threat of communist revolution.
9   Representatives of the corporations Mussolini set up.
10 Italy recognised the Vatican City as a sovereign state and paid for lands taken from the Papal States in 1860–71.
11 It was supposed to replace conflict between employers and workers with co-operation.
12 Land which would have been better suited to dairy or fruit farming was given over to wheat.
13 The lira was over-valued, making Italy's exports uncompetitive.
14 There were subsidies for industry, and under the Corporate State, trade unions were replaced by corporations dominated by the employers.
15 Wages were low and prices high; unemployment was high. But pensions and unemployment benefits were increased.
16 Compensation from Greece. Prestige.
17 Italy, France and Britain jointly condemned German rearmament.
18 Because coal, steel and, above all, oil were excluded from the sanctions.
19 He turned against Britain and France, withdrew from the League of Nations and drew closer to Germany.
20 He made no protest, despite the fact that this brought German troops to the Italian border – unlike his attitude to a similar threat in 1934.

Germany, 1918–45

1   Because the German armies were still in France, so the people thought Germany had lost the war because of the revolution rather than military defeat.
2   By universal suffrage and proportional representation. It controlled taxation and legislation.
3   Proportional representation led to coalition governments.
4   Because the allies did not negotiate it with Germany but presented it for signature.
5   (a) By the army and the freikorps. (b) By a general strike.
6   Because Germany defaulted on its reparations payments.
7   A reduction in reparations payments and an American loan to support the new currency.
8   They lost their savings.
9   Germany accepted the 1919 frontiers with France and Belgium; Britain and Italy guaranteed them.
10 Those who had set up the Weimar Republic in the November Revolution; he blamed them for the 'stab in the back'.
11 It meant taking over land in eastern Europe to provide living space for Germans, and therefore probably meant war.
12 Because they feared communist revolution and because they had lost faith in the Weimar Republic after the currency crisis of 1923.
13 Because it was impossible to form a coalition which commanded a majority in the Reichstag.
14 Brüning, Papen, Schleicher and Hitler.
15 They lost 34 seats in November as compared with July.
16 He had little faith in democracy and was happy to appoint Chancellors of a similar outlook and allow them to rule with the President's emergency powers.
17 It enabled him to play on fears of communism in the election campaign.

18 He excluded Communists under an emergency law after the Reichstag Fire and he did a deal with the Catholic Centre Party.

19 It enabled him to deal with the threat from Röhm and the SA and to keep the loyalty of the army.

20 Co-ordination, i.e. bringing all other organisations under the control of the Nazis.

21 Head of the SS, the police and the Gestapo.

22 Both were Nazi private armies. The SS was an élite body which became immensely powerful. The SA recruited more widely but lost power in the Night of the Long Knives, when its leader, Röhm, was murdered.

23 That their role was to serve the Nazi state as wives and mothers.

24 That the Church would be left in control of its schools in return for dissolving the Catholic Centre Party.

25 All members of the army took an oath of personal loyalty to him.

26 A record of a meeting in which Hitler told his military advisers of his plans for the expansion of Germany.

27 Because they opposed the plans outlined in the Hossbach memorandum; officially, they were dismissed on charges of personal misconduct.

28 Church set up by Protestants who disapproved of the Reich Church set up by the Nazis.

29 Self-sufficiency, to be achieved by boosting domestic production and developing synthetic substitutes for oil and other imports.

30 The Night of Broken Glass – attacks on synagogues and Jewish houses and businesses.

Soviet Russia, 1917–53

1 Industry and banks were nationalised, private trade was forbidden and peasants were required to sell surplus grain to the state at fixed prices.

2 Lenin's secret police.

3 The Political Bureau of the Communist Party, members of which were mainly Commissars. Effectively it ran the government.

4 Fear that the example of revolution would be followed elsewhere; also Britain and France were angry at Russia's desertion of the Allied cause and Lenin's repudiation of foreign debts.

5 Part of White Russia and the Ukraine.

6 Built up the Red Army, which he commanded.

7 They feared the Whites would return the land to the landlords.

8 He realised that War Communism was causing so much discontent that it must be abandoned.

9 Private traders under the New Economic Policy.

10 Stalin, Kamenev and Zinoviev.

11 Trotsky; he meant that Russia should try to bring about revolution throughout the world.

12 Heavy industries such as iron and steel and engineering.

13 Outstanding workers who won prizes for their high production.

14 Russian agriculture was inefficient; production needed to be increased to export more and earn foreign currency; the existence of the kulaks was contrary to communist ideology.

15 Kamenev, Zinoviev, Bukharin, Yagoda, Marshal Tukhachevsky.

16 The People's Commissariat for Internal Affairs, which ran the secret police and organised the purges.

17 Persecuted its priests and closed many churches.

18 Stalin's definition of what the arts should produce – national in form, socialist in content.

19 Eastern Poland, eastern Karelia, the Baltic states.

20 An organisation set up by Stalin to co-ordinate the economies of Russia's Eastern European satellite states.

21 He believed they aimed to overthrow the Communist regime in Russia.

22 To force the western powers to abandon their sectors of Berlin.

Index